SoulSpace

Transform Your Home,
Transform Your Life —
Creating a Home That Is Free
of Clutter, Full of Beauty,
and Inspired by You

Xorin Balbes

**FOREWORD BY
MARIANNE WILLIAMSON**

New World Library
Novato, California

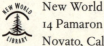 New World Library
14 Pamaron Way
Novato, California 94949

Text design by Tona Pearce Myers

Library of Congress Cataloging-in-Publication Data is available.

First printing, October 2011
ISBN 978-1-60868-037-5
Printed in the United States on 100% postconsumer-waste recycled paper

g New World Library is a proud member of the Green Press Initiative.

10 9 8 7 6 5 4 3 2 1

To my mother,
who let me redecorate her living room when I was seven years old,
and always told me that I would write a book someday.
This one is for her.

*"Create beauty not to excite the senses
but to give sustenance to the soul."*

— Gabriela Mistral

CONTENTS

Part II: Manifesting the Future

Part III: Living the Present

FOREWORD

grew up at 3616 Tartan Lane, in a home my parents built when I was two years old. I didn't know, growing up, that not every family's home was the emotional base camp that 3616 was for us. My parents were world travelers and took their children with them to many exotic places. But there was never any doubt where home was; our house was the beginning and end point of all trips, no matter how great the distances we'd traveled. My father used to say that the best part of a trip was coming home.

Today, while I don't travel the world as extensively as my parents did, I do travel often. And I can't imagine what my life would be if my home were not a place where I could rest, restore, and revitalize in the midst of a hectic schedule. As Xorin Balbes would say in this lovely book, my apartment is my SoulSpace, or spiritual sanctuary. And that makes a tremendous difference in how I experience my life.

This book makes a point that I've lived for myself and believe in passionately: that your home both reflects who you are and can help transform who you are. I've learned that an African artifact can represent a wild and exciting time in my past, that I can place it next to my late grandmother's chaise lounge and be reminded of her love for me, and enjoy sitting on the chaise as I gaze at a photograph of my mother on her wedding day and imbibe her romantic joy. All those things bring harmony to both my heart and my mind. And whether the touchstone in my home is a crystal I wanted with me wherever I lived before I even knew about the power of crystals, or a $5 temple rubbing I bought at a gift shop in Taiwan, I've learned that meaning and money are two separate things. As Xorin says so meaningfully, "This process is a continuous journey of evolution, not acquisition." I have a statue of Buddha from a flower shop in Santa Barbara, who holds in his hands some crystals people have handed me as I've lectured around the world. They remind me of what's important in life, and of how much I have to be grateful for.

I was fortunate during my childhood to have a mother and grandmother as examples of women who treated their homes and the items that were in them lovingly. In the years since, I've been educated further by those whose knowledge has far outdistanced mine — people who could come into my house and politely suggest that the neo-yenta look could use some revising, or that the clutter in my closet was stopping the flow of energy into my career, or that the feng shui of my bedroom was limiting my sex life! One design expert gives you a more sophisticated eye for fabric; another teaches you not to fear white space on the walls. But *SoulSpace* is about more than how we decorate our homes; it's about how we care for ourselves. It guides us into a deeper understanding of more than mere home decoration: it teaches us how to create a home that provides not only for our physical comfort but for our emotional comfort too.

In *SoulSpace*, Xorin reminds us that what all of us yearn for, deep in our hearts, is the experience of home. And when the place we live in is a reflection of our spirit, then we can more easily experience our home within. If all of that sounds wonderful but you have no idea how to *do* it, then read on. Imagine the mythical wizard Merlin as an interior decorator, and you've got Xorin. Imagine a magical treatise on decorating your house, and you've got *SoulSpace*.

This book should be the gift that everyone receives at their housewarming, the book you send to the friend who can't quite get it together in their house or apartment, the book you give politely as a gift to someone who you know is struggling to find peace yet lives in a clanging environment amid clutter or mess. This book is unique and filled with wisdom, not only about design but also about us, not only about beauty but also about transformation, not only about how to decorate your rooms but also about how to better your life.

If you're looking to make your home more reflective of the deepest truths of who you are and what you want in life, then *SoulSpace* is the coolest thing you could possibly read. It takes you, and the home you live in, on a journey toward something beautiful and true. And once there, you really do feel at home — not only in your house or apartment, but also in your soul.

— Marianne Williamson,
author of *The Age of Miracles*

INTRODUCTION

The Eight SoulSpace Stages

Where do you live?

This is one of the most common questions we hear, and we always have a ready answer: "I live on this street, in that neighborhood, in this town or city or country."

I invite you to consider the question in a new way.

Where do you *live*? Where do you feel *alive*? Where do you feel safe, peaceful, hopeful, and supported? Where can you explore your hobbies, think, learn, and love? If your home is just a temporary holding pen where you leave your things during the day instead of a beautiful space that makes you feel safe and calm every time you walk in the door, something is wrong. Your home is more than a place where your possessions are — it is a place where your body can recharge, where your passions can be fulfilled, where you can safely explore yourself and your desires, and where your soul can rest, be inspired, and soar. Home is about satisfying our basic animal needs: eating, sleeping, seeking shelter. But it is also about achieving transcendence on earth through our other needs, the ones that are the basis of our humanity: beauty, love, and creativity.

For the past ten years, I have been redesigning homes with one purpose: to assist the people who live within to create the kind of space where they can flourish instead of just exist. My mission is to weave my wish for peace, beauty, justice, passion, and rejuvenation into all my projects with the intention of inspiring others to live a more soulful, compassionate, and beautiful life.

Consider the following scenarios.

1. As you open the front door, the glow of warm light beckons you inside. You set your bag on a handmade table near the door and slip off your shoes, placing them and your coat in the neatly organized hall closet. The serene, beautifully appointed living room draws you in. You sink deeply in to a soft, comfortable chair and drape a finely knit, cozy throw over your legs. The sky, visible through a large, clear window, is soothing. A feeling of calm and revitalization washes over you. You close your eyes and enjoy the quiet luxury of a catnap before preparing a light supper. You're home.

2. As you open the front door, the knob rattles. It's loose again. The door sticks, and you have to force it open with your shoulder. You make a mental note to call the super. You stumble into the dark hallway as you grope for the light switch. The bulb blows out, leaving you in a gray wash of dim light. The hall closet is crammed to capacity with coats, sweaters, and things you haven't seen in years. You throw your coat on a living room chair instead. The

seat cushion is faded and worn. The air in the room is stale. A feeling of stress and irritation washes over you. You're home. You look around at the clutter and decide to put your coat back on and grab a bite to eat at the local diner.

Where you live and what you live with are an extension of who you are: your living quarters are a physical manifestation of your emotional wants and needs, a mirror of your thoughts, dreams, hopes, wishes, and issues. And it isn't just about the four walls that surround you: it's about the energy with which you fill your space. I want you to consider the possibility that your home is an extension and a physical representation of who you are — and who you have been. Your space holds all your unfinished emotional business and baggage; the interior design of your home is a mirror of the interior design of you.

Thoughts have power. Whether you create your home intentionally or unintentionally, your thoughts and desires have been projected onto the objects that you have purchased, inherited, and collected, and when you see those things, you are consciously or unconsciously reminded of the situations in which they were acquired.

Objects acquired via love make us feel loved. Objects acquired via greed make us feel ashamed. By ridding ourselves of the physical manifestation of negative patterns and surrounding ourselves with positive manifestations of our best selves, we can move forward in an environment designed to help us be our very best.

Transform Your Home, Transform Your Life

Think about an apartment building full of identically shaped apartments that are all the same size, with the same number of rooms and windows. If you were to walk into every one of the identical units in the building, no two would look the same. Each would be colored by its inhabitants. 10A's residents are a forty-something power couple; their apartment has bright red walls and smells of takeout Thai. 10B's young parents have a place full of toys, games, and dust. 10C has only one tenant, an artist in her sixties who listens to Beethoven to drown out the sound of the children next door and has decorated her apartment with plush white carpets and a baby grand piano.

Even though the bare bones of the apartments looked identical when the Realtor sold the units, each unit has been transformed radically by the lives and spirits of the people who live there. Each one has different sights, sounds, smells, and feelings, and each one makes you feel different upon entering. 10A is lively. 10B is chaotic. 10C is serene. The colors, the smells, the sounds, and the entire energy of each space have been transformed by each inhabitant. If you have ever gotten a new roommate, moved in with someone, or had a child — even gotten a pet! — you know that living creatures carry with them a set of habits that color their environments. *Every home tells its own story.*

Your home also has an original story — yours. What messages is your home sending out into the world? This book will help you see what is happening around you right now, really and truly — and it will challenge you to ask yourself if this is who you want to be or if it's time to let go and become a more fully evolved you.

Over the course of my career as a home designer, I have discovered that the process of exploring the interior design of your home can lead to a new and enriched understanding of your real "interior design": the way you think, dream, live, love, and perceive the world.

SoulSpace is the process that I use to transform my home and my life, and the homes and lives of my clients. I came up with the word *SoulSpace* before I had consciously created the eight stages of the SoulSpace process. I had just moved into a new house, which I created very consciously. This conscious design focused on creating a temple instead of just a beautiful show house. I wanted a beautiful home, but more than that, I wanted a sanctuary, a place that would continually remind me and inspire me to be the most amazing example of myself that I could be. When I was finished with the redesign, I didn't have just a space that I could live in. I had a *SoulSpace* that I could grow, learn, live, love, and achieve in, a place where I could truly feel inspired and at peace.

Why must we go to spas to feel relaxed? To hotels or restaurants to feel inspired? We all deserve SoulSpaces — within our own living quarters — that make our senses feel nourished, that make our lives feel fuller and more enriched.

The idea of a SoulSpace stuck with me, and the next time I moved, I paid very close attention to how I was approaching the redesign. I started to break down the process and use it with my clients. It assisted me, it assisted them, and now I pray that it will inspire you to create a home that empowers you to go out into the world and accomplish your dreams, no matter what they are.

How the SoulSpace Process Can Work for You

When you engage in the SoulSpace process, you'll gain insights that bring the following two results.

1. *You'll decode the story that your home is trying to tell you.*
    Whether you were aware of it or not, when you designed your current home, you planted your belief system, your

desires, your wishes, your issues, and many other things that affect whether you achieve your goals and dreams. Using your space as a cue, you can begin to take a deeper look at many areas of your life and open up to new possibilities.

Imagine a bachelor with a picture of his college girlfriend in his bedroom, a banker with an easel under the bed, a teacher with seating for one in her apartment. It's no surprise that the bachelor wonders why he isn't luckier in love, the banker wishes he still had time to paint, and the teacher hopes to make new friends. In each of these cases, the space itself reflects the areas of lack in the inhabitant's life. Through the SoulSpace process, you'll uncover what your home says about you.

2. *You'll redesign or reassign your space to support the person you truly are or would like to become.* Once you make space, physically and figuratively, you will have more room to imagine what you would like to have in your life, and you'll have the physical space to manifest those desires by actually creating rooms or areas in which they can flourish. By clearing out the "noise" in your home, you will be able to hear the whispers within you and give them voice. By consciously designing your space with a high level of intention, you will infuse each action and object with that intention.

What would happen if the bachelor got rid of the photograph and understood that he was holding on — and why he was holding on? What would happen if the banker cleared a comfortable space for painting and started expressing his creativity? What else in his life might open up? What if the teacher got a few more chairs and invited some colleagues over for a cocktail? If she made space for more love in her home, how might her everyday experience of life change?

How to Feel at Home When You're at Home

We all need a refuge. We all want to live in a space that makes us feel safe, inspired, fully refreshed, and ready to take on the world. We all deserve to live in a place that we can truly call home. Unfortunately, for many of us, the condition and appearance of the place where we live make us feel uneasy instead of refreshed, resulting in relationship, career, and creative blocks. With all the vulnerability in our world today, now more than ever we need to feel truly at home in our living quarters and in our own bodies. *It is time for all of us to come home.*

When you intentionally create a space that promotes growth and change, you support a natural process. We are all always growing and changing, and we can either fight it or embrace it and encourage it. When you promote positive changes by employing conscious design, you are seeding your home with wishes and desires for your life. The right environment encourages you to embody your greatness, inspiring personal revolution and evolution, gently urging you toward achievement, greater success, and the life that you were meant to live — toward the greatest expression of your soul.

SoulSpace will teach you how to listen to the messages encoded in the home you have created. You'll then be empowered to re-create your space to support the life you have always dreamed of living. Once you face your belongings, confront your fears, unclutter your space, and discover your personal desires and truths, you will have more energy, feel more inspired, access more creativity, and find that you can harness your creativity and find refuge, renewal, and splendor within your own four walls.

By working through the process in manageable stages, you deepen your understanding of yourself as you emotionally dismantle and physically renovate your surroundings. By using your belongings as a concrete way to investigate and understand your feelings and attachments, you will expose and then begin to break down old patterns, literally "making room" for your new, more evolved self.

If you can achieve and anchor beauty in your most sacred and intimate refuge — your home — you will find that your home will support you in every area of your life; if you can create peace and beauty in your home, you can create peace and beauty in all the areas of your life and in all the spaces you inhabit.

The Eight Stages

The SoulSpace process has eight stages, broken down into three parts, that will take you on a step-by-step journey through what may be one of the most important projects of your life. By using conscious design with the SoulSpace process, you can learn to support yourself in a whole new way, learning to be the person you want to become tomorrow, supported by the experiences of yesterday, living more fully in who you are today.

Part 1 focuses on *knowing the past*, because the past is what brought us to where we are and made us who we are right now. When we investigate our conscious and unconscious attachments to the past by looking clearly at the things we have chosen to own and the home we have organized for ourselves, we can learn to honor those parts of ourselves that we may have forgotten, and release the extra baggage — literal and metaphorical — that we have been carrying around for too many years. It's about becoming aware of all the choices we have made leading up to this moment, and deciding whether we want to continue making the same choices as we move forward.

Part 1 comprises the first three stages of the SoulSpace process. In stage 1, ASSESS, we examine how and why we have created the home we have, and we take an accurate reading of what and whom it supports. Stage 2, RELEASE, teaches us how to let go and why doing so is integral. This stage culminates in our disposing of literal and figurative baggage. In stage 3, CLEANSE, we clean and purify our home, paying homage to our most cherished memories and belongings. This stage awakens our gratitude for the things we love.

Part 2 is about *manifesting the future*. It invites us to ask ourselves, "How do I want to live?" During this phase we focus on our hopes for the future, learning how to lay the foundation for our dreams via the objects we choose to live with. We work to make changes in our homes that will trigger continued change and growth in our everyday activities so that our environment can gently whisper to us and remind us of our chosen path.

Stages 4 through 6 make up part 2. In stage 4, DREAM, we let our imaginations soar as we brainstorm the ways in which we can employ our home in the manifestation of our dreams. Then, in stage 5, DISCOVER, we collect the ingredients for realizing our dreams; we go out into the world to be inspired, opening ourselves to what the world delivers. Stage 6, CREATE, helps us manifest our dreams in three dimensions by infusing our home with furnishings that reflect our true selves.

Part 3 is *living the present*. Here we take steps to live actively in the now, with a full understanding of what has brought us here and of our goals for the future. We can begin to live life in harmony with our true nature and in an environment that supports and encourages us to continuously live our dreams.

Stage 7, ELEVATE, encourages us to nourish all our senses and make living in our home a richer experience. Finally, in stage 8, we CELEBRATE! Now that we have a SoulSpace to enjoy every day, we can share more of ourselves with our friends and family.

Inspiring Change through Conscious Design

Your SoulSpace is not defined by expensive things or perfectly matched furnishings. It isn't about your budget or your grasp of aesthetics. No matter how big or small your space is, your Soul-Space can reflect who you are, what you love, where you want to go, and who you will become. Your home can be your greatest support, inspiring you daily and reminding you of your deepest desires.

As an award-winning interior designer, I beautify architecturally significant buildings and the homes of my clients to media acclaim. And there's another side to the work I do. As a spiritual seeker, I go beyond aesthetics to help people identify the beauty that they can have around them, and the beauty that exists within them.

My own home, Sowden House in Los Feliz, California, is an example of Mayan- and Aztec-influenced modern architecture. It was designed in 1926 by Lloyd Wright, the son of Frank Lloyd Wright. It was a mess when I purchased it in 2002, and I spent the year restoring it to its former glory, adding furnishings and other elements that would both honor Lloyd Wright's vision and create a SoulSpace I could truly live my life in. Once the restoration was complete, Sowden House served as a set for Martin Scorsese's film *The Aviator*, among others.

Restoring Sowden House helped me understand my potential and my possibilities, and started connecting me to a larger world than the one I was living in. Now, nearly a decade later, I am involved in a major renovation project of my property on Maui, where I am working alongside roofers, contractors, and experts in local vegetation. This development process is forcing me to once again examine who I am, what I stand for, and how I would like to lead my life. My houses have always reflected my personal journey. I have lived in over thirty homes, and each space has acted as a mirror, showing me where I have been and where I can go, revealing another layer of my experience and my soul.

I am writing this book because I hope to inspire you to live a fuller, more realized life, beginning with your home and the interior design of your soul and then expanding that consciousness into every area of your life. As I write this book, as I encourage you to create your true SoulSpace, I am once again re-creating my space, and re-creating myself.

Making space for our soul's growth encourages external change and growth. As the workers around me dig holes and pull out trees, I remind myself that soon this scene of chaos is going to give way to a scene of ultimate serenity. Only by engaging in the chaos now will I later be able to sit in utter repose. Only by truly understanding what I ultimately want to do in my space can I understand what I need to do with the space now; only by truly understanding the space within myself can I create the ideal space to nurture and inspire me.

And I don't just mean choosing the right trees or buying the right furniture, though those things are a big part of the beauty that this place will become. I mean investing in the space in a truly personal way. For example, when I first bought this land, I buried a number of stones on the property. I had collected these stones throughout my life on my travels around the world, taking one from each place where I'd had profound and life-changing experiences. By integrating the stones into my new home, I transformed them into stepping stones that link my past to my future.

Connect the Dots to See the Bigger Picture

As you read this book, I encourage you to find and connect to those pieces of your past that are useful for your present and future, and cast out all the weight that anchors you to past pains so that you can be free to move forward. Once you understand the relationship of your physical space and objects to your emotional attachments and limitations, you can identify what no longer serves you, let go of it, and then create space for growth in your life and your home.

This process is a continuous journey of evolution, not acquisition. It is about understanding the consciousness behind all your choices and using that power to change your life. Here's what I tell my clients, and what I'm going to tell you: *Transform your SoulSpace at your soul's pace*. This is an *active* process; it isn't a *forced* process. You can redesign — or reassign — one room at a time, or your entire home. You can do it in a month or a year. The important thing is not how quickly you go; it's that you start! Be present with each choice, and make everything you choose something that inspires you and truly feels beautiful to you.

Part of being present entails being honest with what is in this moment and understanding your needs, your means, and your abilities. A tennis court you will never use will not enhance your SoulSpace. An oven range you can't afford will not enhance your SoulSpace. And renovating a farmhouse by yourself — because it sounded awesome when you read about it in a magazine, even though you have never held a drill before — is not the path to your true SoulSpace.

Asking for help is a big one when it comes to SoulSpacing. Many of us feel as if we have to do everything ourselves, for myriad reasons — we feel either that we will do it best or that we don't want to bother anyone. Sometimes we assume that others are too busy to help us. Or that we will appear too needy. Whether the help you need is personal or professional, please, don't hesitate to reach out.

As you work your way through the book, no matter what stage you are in, if you need help, ask for it! For example, for stage 1, ASSESS, you can ask a trusted friend or relative to do a "walkabout" with you. You can also ask your therapist or counselor if they would consider an at-home session that focused on your belongings. That said, this is a participatory sport. Simply hiring a host of experts to do all the thinking and planning for you isn't going to help you get your best self set up. On the other hand, working collaboratively *with* experts who understand architecture, remodeling, and contracting can be a great way to create your dreams at home.

Embarking on the Journey

SoulSpace is a book about the interior design of your space that extends to the interior design of your soul. A beautiful home can be just a shell; I want your home to be a beautiful reflection of your truest self, a safe place where your soul can flourish. This is real interior design — we aren't just moving tables and chairs, or choosing the most fashionable color of paint; we are investigating our deepest challenges, desires, and attachments by examining *how the way we have assembled our homes provides clues to the way we have organized our lives.*

If you have picked up this book, you are ready to reevaluate your choices and begin anew.

When I work with a client, before we begin the SoulSpace process we take a moment to connect with the journey that we are about to undertake. So before you begin your SoulSpace journey, take a few moments to really consider what you are about to do and why. You might want to read this affirmation aloud:

As I begin my SoulSpace journey, I will allow myself to truly see where I am living and who I truly am. I give myself permission to really see the space that I live in, and the emotional connections I have to all the objects and furniture in my space. I wish to see where I am blocked and where I am free, where I am stuck and where I need to let go. Without judgment, I will heal my home and I will heal myself. I desire to live authentically, and I am ready to live my dreams. My past is a part of me, but it does not define me. I will cherish the memories that serve me, and I will release the regrets that hold me back. Right now, I am consciously taking the wheel. I will re-create my space as I reconnect with myself.

Remember, if there are things missing from your life, there's a good chance they are reflected in the space in which you live. If there are issues that you have been holding on to, you will likely see them represented in the objects and the space in your home as well. Your home has been speaking to you for years. If you look and listen very carefully, you will hear what it has been saying to you.

My Wish for You

My definition of *beautiful* is a space where you can be yourself to the fullest. The time is now! Whether your home is full of Danish modern or Ikea, teak from Thailand or grandma's favorite antiques — no matter your personal style, no matter where you live or what your income — SoulSpace is your unique process of self-discovery, helping you identify problem areas and understand, access, and create your dreams.

If you want to paint, you need a place to paint. If you want to play your guitar or learn to play the piano, you need an instrument and a place to put it. What is the use of having a sewing room if what you really need is an office? Why have a TV room when what you really need is an exercise room? Even in small spaces, creating nooks and corners that inspire focused activities is more than possible: it is what will make your home unique and perfect for you. Express yourself in all ways in your space. If you can't do it at home, you won't be able to do it anywhere.

The SoulSpace process is a step-by-step experience that will teach you how to embrace the space you inhabit. Your home is not just your castle — it is your altar, your temple, your SoulSpace. A place where your soul along with your body can rest and rejuvenate before you go back out into the world to live and create your dreams. A place where your creativity — your love of cooking, of music, of art, of physical fitness — can be nourished and encouraged.

My wish for you is to live in beauty, in your home and in your life — the kind of beauty that works for *you*.

PART I

Knowing the Past

"You have to know the past in order to understand the present."

—— DR. CARL SAGAN

STAGE 1: ASSESS

STAGE 2: RELEASE

STAGE 3: CLEANSE

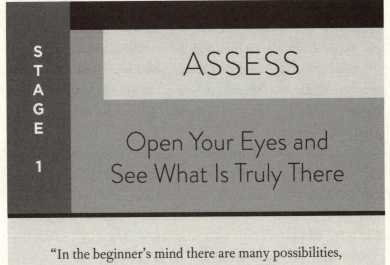

STAGE 1

ASSESS

Open Your Eyes and See What Is Truly There

"In the beginner's mind there are many possibilities,
but in the expert's there are few."

— SHUNRYU SUZUKI-ROSHI

People who practice Zen talk about "beginner's mind." This is the magical ability to see things anew even if we've experienced them a million times before. In order to fully assess the space you live in, you're going to need to cultivate your beginner's mind so you can truly see and feel the space you have created. The world we live in teaches us that experts are always better, and we all appreciate the value of an experienced opinion every time we consult a physician or an attorney. Sometimes, though, we must remember that with too much experience, the world of possibility often becomes crowded out. *Can't* replaces *can*. *Won't* takes the place of *will*.

Today we're going to try to take a beginner's look at something we probably consider ourselves experts on: ourselves. Do you really know yourself as well as you think you do? Or have you been ignoring things that bother you for weeks or months or even years? Do you see where you are getting in your own way, where you are creating situations that hold you back from what you really desire?

The journey you are about to begin has the power to change your life — if you are ready and willing to engage fully with the process. The book you are holding contains the tools to deepen your understanding of your own needs as you create a home that will fully support the life you want to lead. Being 100 percent present and open is the only way to get all the possible benefits from each of the SoulSpace stages.

The ASSESS phase is where you will do the important detective work that will enable you to create growth and change both inside and out. Use your beginner's mind to take a fresh look at what you've become immune to seeing; appraise what is there on a physical and emotional level, learn to appreciate the best of what exists, and begin to recognize what no longer serves you in your life.

What Is Your Home Trying to Tell You?

Lili is a successful woman who owns her beautiful home, but when she called me, she sounded frustrated and hopeless. She was happy with her life at work, but she was not really settled and happy with her life at home. She had tried several times to redesign her home; still, she could never get it right — all she was doing was moving her furniture around. So she reached out to me to see what we could do to change the situation.

When I arrived, we sat down and talked for a while before walking around the house looking for clues to what was working and to her unhappiness. She explained to me that purchasing the home had been a big symbol to her that she had "arrived." It turned out that she realized upon moving in that she was lonely in the space she had created. She had entered a new phase of her life, and she wanted to go from being an "I" to being part of a "we."

She had the home, and she wanted to share it with someone. Attractive and lively, Lili often dated, yet none of her relationships seemed to stick. After a string of failed attempts at love, she had just about given up.

Lili takes good care of what she owns, and everything I saw was tidy and in its place. On the surface, it all looked okay. I kept looking. I wanted to understand what was happening beneath the surface.

As we moved through her home, assessing and observing, I noticed that her home and her life were perfectly set up — for one person. Lili's king-size bed was pushed up against the wall, which would have made it awkward for a second person to get in and out comfortably. The living room featured a couch that was gorgeous — and awkward to sit on. It faced away from the entryway and therefore was very unwelcoming, floating in the middle of the room like a ship at sea. Once seated, I was still very conscious of the vast space behind me, and I kept turning around to make sure nobody was there.

I asked Lili how she felt on that couch. "I don't know," she told me. "I usually just sit in that chair." The chair was soft and luxurious. I could see why she liked it. I could also see that there wasn't room for anybody but her to feel comfortable in that house.

Decode the Message

I asked her why she thought she still didn't have the love she wanted. She said that she didn't know. I asked her when she had last had a lover over. She thought about it. "Not for a while," she said. "In my last relationship, we usually ended up staying at his house, and he lived out of town."

I knew that Lili loved her house and dreamed of settling in it with a partner. I wanted her to see what I saw: her house was big enough for four but comfortable only for one. We walked back into the bedroom.

"Lili," I said, "what do you see when you look around this room?"

"A room," she said. "Just…a bedroom."

"How many people can get in and out of that bed comfortably?" I asked her.

"One," she said. We walked into the living room.

"How many comfortable chairs are there in this room?" I asked.

"One," she said, starting to get my point.

In the kitchen, there was a bistro table with only one chair. "I thought that having two chairs would make me feel like someone was missing," she said, "that it would make me feel lonely."

"How does one chair make you feel?" I asked.

"Lonely," she admitted.

I encouraged her to consider finding a new place for dining, one with a bigger table that would create space for companionship and love. The extra seating would be like a placeholder for the people she would invite into her life, holding the space for what was to come.

As we moved around the house, identifying all the places where she could create space to invite someone else in, Lili began to realize that perhaps the reason she didn't have men over was that there really wasn't room for them. When she took a fresh look at her space, she was able to see that what had seemed logical

— creating a space for one person since she was only one person — didn't leave any room for the possibility that she would soon have another person in her life. She had unconsciously organized her personal space to support her single life.

Over the course of our discussions, Lili realized that her "single-mindedness" went way beyond furniture. She was always on guard, she told me, afraid that people might be attracted to her for her money and not for what she could offer them on a deeper level. This fear translated into purposely organizing her large house so that only she could be comfortable there. She now recognized that by making room in her home, she could also make room inside her. Trusting that the right person would enter her life — trusting that she could find someone to really love her — was a key element in our eventual redesign. As we uncovered her fears and hesitations, we also made plans to counter them by imbuing her space with a sense of openness and sharing.

Create Your Dreams

Using ASSESS to identify the way Lili had been approaching her life helped us focus our redesign.

During the RELEASE phase, we got rid of her one chair and bistro table in preparation for the larger, more companionable dining set to come. We also made note that we needed to move both her bed away from the wall and the sofa to a more welcoming location, so that everybody in her home would have a safe-feeling space in which to relax.

In the CLEANSE phase, while going through some old boxes, she found some photos of herself looking pretty and put one of them in a central place as a reminder of what an attractive, desirable woman she was.

DREAM allowed her to focus on the intention behind this renovation: to create a home where others could feel cherished and welcomed, and to feel her true, open nature instead of living like a guarded woman as she'd been doing. To that end, she decided that she wanted two comfortable sitting chairs instead of just the one. Since she loved to read and hoped to find a partner who shared that quiet joy, she asked that we make sure to provide enough light to make reading an enjoyable experience for both of them. Our redesign always kept two in mind.

In the DISCOVER phase, she looked for lamps that gave light in two directions, and when we found her perfect seating, she knew it immediately. Instead of looking in the big-name department stores as Lili used to do, we focused our attention on romantic-looking period furniture at consignment shops and auctions. The velvet chairs we found made Lili feel like "falling in love." Since this was what we were aiming for, I knew that the chairs were perfect. Other pieces we got that were directly related to the clues we discovered during the assessment included a romantically inclined breakfast nook for two and two nightstands and two lamps. We prepared her home for companionship, trusting that if she opened her space up, love would come calling. We made sure that the space was inviting and available for someone else to step into. Starting with Lili's desires, we were able to design and create with those needs specifically in mind.

By listening to the message that was coded in the way her home was organized — what the ASSESS phase is all about — and focusing her redesign accordingly, Lili was able to make a huge breakthrough in her romantic life. Physically making room for someone else made her realize that she also had to make room in her heart. Being able to see the truth of where she really was allowed her to consciously make a necessary shift to bring the interior design of her soul and the exterior design of her home into sync.

It didn't take long before both comfy chairs were occupied and both nightstands were stacked with books.

Big Is Not Always Better

When Barbra came to me, she was convinced that the reason her marriage was falling apart was that her husband, Scott, didn't trust her enough to decorate the massive home they had just bought. This was the first "grown-up" home they had owned together — and it was too big for them, she said. She and Scott had been living in a small cottage with their two children, and everything had been fine. Then, as did many people during the real estate boom, they had upgraded to the house of their dreams, or so they thought. The house, an imposing structure with a white picket fence on a huge plot of land in a neatly landscaped suburb, was everything Barbra had always thought she wanted. It was supposed to make them feel successful, but instead it left them feeling incompetent.

The grand scale of the house was an issue from the get-go. Scott didn't think Barbra could design the house on her own, so he hired a designer, who completely took over the process, recommending everything from color and textures to what the living areas should be used for. The designer painted everything a muddy brown color that Barbra hated (Barbra had a choice word for what it reminded her of, which I'll leave you to guess).

A year later, the house was still unfinished. They felt "stuck in the mud." The couple heard about me at a party and decided to put in a call for help.

They hated the house, and their relationship was on the rocks.

As soon as Scott had hired the designer, Barbra had felt as if he didn't trust her. And as soon as she felt that way, things went from bad to worse. The house was making them miserable, and with the dip in the economy, there was no way they could sell it and move on to a home that suited them better. For the sake of their children, they were "trying to make it work." What that really meant, said Barbra, practically in tears, was that the two were living like strangers who happened to share the same kids. Because the house had plenty of extra bedrooms, Scott and she were living in separate rooms. The only thing they ever talked about was the kids, whom they always cared for separately. None of their friends knew what was going on, but Barbra's mother had noticed that her daughter was no longer wearing her wedding rings.

Look for the Positive

When I started working with the pair, our assessment focused first on finding the things they liked, things they could come together on to begin the process of trying to bring them back together. The problem with their home wasn't the decor — it was well decorated, though perhaps not to everybody's taste. And the problem wasn't that it was too small, as so many of us think about our spaces. And the issue wasn't even that it was too big, which was what Barbra chose to focus on. The problem was that they weren't creating it *together*. Their home had become a symbol of their separateness instead of their union, and of their differences instead of their similarities. I was convinced that it would take a feeling of togetherness in the design of their home to bring about a closer union between these two obviously unhappy people.

As we moved through the home, it was amazing to me that

there was *nothing* that they agreed on. If Scott liked a painting, Barbra hated it. If Barbra loved a piece of art, Scott thought it would be better served as fodder for the fireplace. Finally, I turned to them and asked point-blank, "Isn't there anything that you both like?"

After some hesitation, Barbra went to the closet and pulled out a quilt that was woven of blues and greens, all the colors of the sky and sea.

"Wow! I completely forgot about that quilt we bought in Santa Fe," said Scott. "It's gorgeous!"

"I think it's beautiful," said Barbra.

After hours of interacting, this was the first time that I saw them agree on anything, and the first time I saw them smile at each other, just a little. They had locked up in a closet the parts of themselves that they shared and trusted in each other — it was time to open up all the doors and let the light in and the love out.

This was the beginning of their working together. They needed one thing that they could agree on so they could continue the process and collaborate as a team to transform their space. They finally had a touchstone, an item that they agreed on, that they could continue to come back to during the rest of the process when they were not in agreement...and many times they had to do just that.

Quit the Blame Game and Embrace Your Space

If you believe that all your problems stem from the physical dimensions of your space, or the fact that you rent instead of own, or own a suburban home when you'd prefer to rent a loft downtown, think again. I hear some version of the following comments time and time again.

"I'm stressed because my apartment is too small. I don't have the room to do what I need."

"We can't decorate this place because it's just too huge. No matter how many pieces we bring in, it never feels like home."

"I'm a renter, so it doesn't make sense to make the improvements this place needs to work."

"If I had another room…"

"If I had more windows…"

All of these are basically excuses. And you've got to let them go if you're going to see the truth beneath the surface. Wherever you are, it is time to move into more of you and connect to yourself more intimately in your home.

I'm certainly not suggesting that if you live in a one-room basement apartment with no windows, you wouldn't feel more comfortable in a duplex with three terraces. Yet the dimensions of your space can't be blamed for all the problems; this just keeps you from seeing what is really going on. Think about it like this: If Scott and Barbra can be so miserable with an excess of bedrooms, who's to say bigger would really make you feel any better? No matter how small or big your space is, there is always room to move more of yourself into every nook and cranny.

Chances are, you're not in a situation that would allow you to abandon the space you've been blaming and move into a better one. However, if there's something in your life that's really bothering you, I'm not convinced that moving would even help as much as you imagine — you'd bring all your baggage with you into the new space. So it's time to stop the ifs and buts, bid adieu to the excuses, and make your space your own. You have to embrace where you are right now in order to find yourself in a better space, both inside yourself and outside.

Beware of Beauty

Getting your home just right isn't always about having the most beautiful items. What about the feelings behind each belonging? Where did it come from? Who does it remind you of? Why do you cherish it? Just because something would fetch a high price at an auction doesn't make it a prize. During the assessment, I want you to cast your eye below the surface as you consider your belongings.

Take Linda, an amazing, confident woman who was a friend as well as a client. I knew Linda before she was married and during her five-year marriage. When the relationship ended, something about Linda changed: she just didn't seem like the same woman anymore. I couldn't put my finger on it, so when she invited me to her home for lunch so we could discuss her upcoming renovation, I was excited to connect with her on her own turf, where I could try to make sense of what had happened to her.

As we moved through her apartment during the assessment, she seemed very connected to all her things. I couldn't figure out what the problem was. Then we walked into the living room, where she led me directly to a gorgeous painting hanging front and center in the room.

She explained to me that this was her most prized possession. I totally understood: it was absolutely magnificent — something I would be proud to hang in my home.

Then she explained how she had gotten it. She had "won" the painting in her divorce, and she bragged to me about how she had gotten even by getting his favorite thing. She thought it was a symbol of her independence. But as we talked, I realized that this lovely painting was an anchor to her past that was triggering distressing memories each time she passed it. The painting held all the unconscious and unresolved anger she still had about her past relationship.

Not Just What — Why

The assessment phase is where you really need to consider what you love and *why* you love it, what you dislike and *why* you dislike it, what rooms in your house make your feel at home, and which ones make you feel like a stranger in your own home. You need to take inventory of your actual belongings and their organization within your home, as well as the feelings that you have attached to all those things.

For some of us, an expensive portrait by a master might be just the thing to invigorate us with creative excitement every time we walk by it. For Linda, a similar painting was a reminder of her failed marriage and the revenge that turned out to be less satisfying than it would have been to just move on. Linda wasn't reveling in her revenge — she was stuck in her divorce. She wasn't just holding on — she was being held back.

She sold the painting and used the money to begin her renovation and her new life at home by buying another piece of art that made her feel refreshed and uplifted. Instead of using the expensive old painting as a bridge to her painful recent past, she used it as a bridge to a brighter future. This is what we must strive to do with all the things that no longer serve us. The new painting reminds Linda that she is a powerful individual, whereas the old one linked her to a situation where she had felt abandoned and resentful. Since then, she tells me, some of her anger toward her ex has abated, and she has even begun dating again.

Take Emotional Inventory

As you begin the process of figuring out what you want your space to look and feel like, and who you want to be, it's important to take inventory of where you really are right now, in this moment. I don't mean just a physical inventory of the actual furnishings. I mean an emotional inventory of what is attached to each object. By decoding the emotional and mental projections that cling to each item in your home, and defining the expectations that your interior design creates for you, you can begin to transform yourself along with your space.

Look around with fresh eyes and see what you have collected over time. Do your things really excite you? Some may remind you of a time in your life that you are no longer attached to. The things we save can be powerful anchors to unpleasant memories, feelings, or places that we should be letting go of instead of keeping close. These things have been placeholders waiting for you to feel the emotions and release them when you are ready. Make sure not to judge yourself for where you have been and what you are still holding on to; that judgment would only contribute to keeping you stuck where you are. Self-forgiveness and self-love are the only way through.

Consider the Deeper Meaning

During the first assessment I did with Marsha, a woman I'd met in an art class, I noticed that she had a wedding dress hanging in her closet. I thought she was single, so I asked her about it.

"I was married for a year when I was twenty," she told me. "We married too young, and it didn't work out. Still, we were high school sweethearts, and I have such wonderful memories of those times."

The two were still friends, and she had even gone to his wedding a few years prior. But, as I pointed out to her, he had moved on, and she had not. She even had the matching shoes that she had worn down the aisle more than ten years earlier.

She insisted to me that by holding on to these items she was holding on not to her marriage but to the real love that they had shared in their youth.

"I want to remember the good parts, not the bad parts," she said. I wasn't buying it. I still wasn't convinced that keeping that dress in the closet was a good idea, especially since it was hanging in a rather prominent place where it was immediately visible every time she glanced in the closet. Even if she was looking in the closet for the perfect little dress to wear on a date, the first thing she would see was that white dress. Was it really a memory of happier times?

"When is the last time you tried on that dress?" I asked her.

"Not since I was married," she said.

I encouraged her to put it on to see how it made her feel. She said she would think about it; a week after I left her home, I still hadn't heard from her again.

The truth is that not everybody is ready to see through the clouds to the bright sunshine beyond. We are so scared that when we let go of the pain and the mediocre elements of our home, they will be replaced by nothing, or perhaps by something worse. We don't see that holding on keeps us from knowing and experiencing our true natures.

In some cases, the purpose of the ASSESS phase is to uncover and remember those objects that lift us up. At the same time that we are cherishing objects that weigh us down, we are ignoring exactly those objects that contain the keys to our self-confidence and our self-knowledge. So often we are on automatic pilot. Slow down and take a breath. Let yourself see and feel what is really there. Truly consider what is in front of you, one step, one feeling, one object at a time. There's no rush!

Display Your Accomplishments with Pride

One lovely afternoon a few weeks after I met my partner, Jason, who is now such a big part of my life, we were spending time at his apartment at the beach. He was reading on the couch, and I was poking around in the apartment — with his permission, of course — trying to learn more about this man from his things. At the bottom of the closet, I discovered an award hidden under a pile of stuff.

"What's this?" I asked.

"Just an award," he said, downplaying it.

"An award for what?"

"Best Newcomer to Broadway," he said. Jason had gotten the award for his very successful performance in a Broadway show. Of course, given my obsession with the connection between people and things, I wanted him to put it in a much more conspicuous place, where all could see it and enjoy what it represented: his talent.

By the time I left that day, I had placed the award on his desk as a visible token of his past successes, and he had agreed to leave it there. Just a few weeks later, his agent called with two opportunities, one in a television show and one in a movie. Jason went after them with enthusiasm and confidence. Was it because we had moved that award? Who knows. A few weeks after that, the calls came in — he had landed both roles!

Four years later, Jason and I were spending most of our time at my house, but the award was still in his beach apartment. I encouraged him to bring the award to our home, where he could see it every day and really connect to his successful life as a star performer, so he did. This had the added result of making me feel that he trusted me enough to house his ambitions and successes in our shared home. This time, neither of us was surprised when shifting the location of the award helped spark a shift in consciousness that, in turn, touched off key incidents. What did this mean for Jason? Soon after we moved the award to our home, he was invited to be a producer for a critically acclaimed Broadway show. What did this mean for me? Of course, I got to say, "I told you so!"

That is the power of the objects we choose to have around us. It is so important to seed our environments with things that speak to us and support us in all we are capable of being.

Assessing Your Home: Insight in Action

The assessment process means taking a long look at your home. Start by putting on beautiful music that inspires you. Go outside and close the front door, then step inside. Usually when you come in, you probably drop your keys by the door and rush through to eat, to take care of things, or to watch TV. When was the last time you really looked at all your things and thought about how your home makes you feel? How long has it been since you put any attention into your home and the things in it? When was the last time you touched and loved each object in your home?

Take a good look at your space — and then think about it.

Meditate on it. Reflect on it. No judgment — just observation. As you move around, I'd like you to first pay attention to the obvious elements — after layout and colors, you'll think about the furniture. Then consider the accessories: the pictures on the walls or the vases on the tables. Then dig deeper, looking under the beds, in the drawers, and in all the closets.

As you stroll slowly through the house, consider the questions and suggestions listed in the sections below, paying attention to the big picture as well as the details. In the ASSESS phase, you don't have to worry about making changes yet. You just have to identify the areas that need your loving care. You are beginning to plumb the depths of your mind for enlightenment. Moving the couches will come later, don't worry!

As ideas pop into your mind, write them down so you can refer back to them later. Don't be too concerned with answering every question or making long lists of precisely what you will do in your home. Simply note the strongest feelings you have, particularly if it is clear that there are things you absolutely want to get rid of or cherish more.

Don't rush through this phase. Take it one room, one closet, or one cabinet at a time if you need to. Again, I want you to create your SoulSpace at your soul's pace. Self-awareness doesn't usually strike us overnight, so be patient. And remember: the ASSESS phase is not an exam or a true-or-false quiz. There are no right or wrong answers, only a series of opportunities for you to adopt beginner's mind so you can truly see your belief systems, unresolved issues, imagined limitations, and the opportunities for change and growth that exist within your home.

It's time to get present by completing the cycle of the past and determining what you truly love and want to continue having in your life — and what to let go of — so you can move into your future, supported instead of encumbered by your past.

FOCUSING ON LAYOUT AND INTENTION

We sometimes feel that if only we had a newer home, or a home that had been in our family for years, or a larger home, or a smaller home, then all our problems would magically go away. Of course, that's never the case. And blaming the space is just another excuse. What excuses do you make for being unhappy in your home — too big? too small? too much stuff? not enough? Each space comes with its own challenges — our job is to identify them and lay them to rest through balanced, careful planning.

Just because it's a bedroom now doesn't mean it has to stay that way forever. Consider each room individually and evaluate its use and necessity in your life and home. Then make sure you're taking full advantage of the space and consider how it might be better used.

Which room do you use the most? Why? *This will help you decide how to focus your resources.*

Is there a room you never use? Is your garage well used? How about outdoor areas? What are you missing? What do you not need? *Wasted space can become a place where you can achieve your dreams: turn a never-used office into a yoga studio or an art studio, or a spare bedroom into an office.*

Is there a flow from room to room? What rooms connect to each other? Are entrances blocked with furniture? *If you can't move about easily, this will be a key area to focus on. Where might you have blocks in other areas of your life that can be shifted for better flow?*

Are eating areas clean and neat and a pleasure to enjoy a nice meal in? *Keep trash cans and recycling bins out of sight, if possible. Our surroundings affect our experiences; let's make those experiences as "nourishing" as we can.*

Are sleeping areas messy and full of reminders of work instead of life and love? *Keep bedrooms for romance and relaxation and banish work to another area of your home.*

Are shared areas truly communal? Do they foster conversation and intimacy? Or are couches placed for impact instead of intimate conversation? *Reflect on how people gather in your home to see which seating areas work the best. A big table or extra-comfy living room can improve relationships and communication. Creating nooks for conversation and shared activities can do wonders to bring people together. Create more intimacy at home, and you will become more intimate in the world.*

Does your home feel cramped? *Get rid of the excess; clutter makes small spaces feel even smaller, and your soul needs space in which to breathe, rest, and rejuvenate.*

FOCUSING ON COLOR: USING WHAT'S THERE AS THE MUSE FOR YOUR INSPIRATION

During my renovations in Maui, I worked very hard to find the right color for the main buildings. I wanted them to be a part of the landscape in a way that was vibrant but still natural; I didn't want them to blend in and become invisible, but I didn't want them to dominate.

While walking the property, keeping my eyes open and using my beginner's mind, I stopped working so hard to find the right color. Right then I discovered the perfect color. How is this possible? By just walking and seeing, I was able to see the inspiration that had eluded me. Almost every day, I had walked by the same trees, the same grove of bananas. But this time, I assessed: I really *looked*. Then the land stepped forward to assist me in choosing the color.

When I looked closely at the beautiful banana flowers hanging in the orchard, I was struck by the color of the leaf, a deep reddish-purple that stirred me to my very soul. The color of the leaf moved me so deeply that I knew it was to be the color of the buildings.

Oftentimes, the natural environment that surrounds a home offers clues to what the color of the home should be. Inside your home, you'll want to pay attention to the colors that abound and see how they move you.

There are all the traditional ways to look for inspiration, such as with color samples and swatches, but often our deepest, truest style is living in some object in our homes — say, a piece of clothing, piece of jewelry, painting, or picture.

What colors are prominent? How do they make you feel? Happy? Peaceful? Do they bring up old memories? Do they remind you of other places you have been?

Do you keep your favorite flowers in a vase? What color are they? What texture are they? Do they remind you of springtime, summer, winter, or fall? *Experiment by putting various flowers and different colors together. What works together and what doesn't? Create a simple bouquet to inspire you.*

Did you choose the paint colors, or were they selected by the ex-roommate who left on bad terms?

REFLECTING PERSONAL STYLE

While magazines and books might sometimes make you think otherwise, style isn't about this year's colors or next year's fabrics. It isn't about copying the latest lines or mimicking a celebrity's posh pad. Style is about figuring out what colors, textures, and designs make you feel relaxed, inspired, uplifted, and ready to live your life to the fullest. I go through my clients' closets with them and have them point out all the clothing that they love and feel looks great on them. Often the style in their clothing — whether it is modern, conservative, or traditional — is the right choice for them in their home environment. It's not about being perfect. It's about getting personal. Who is it that has been hiding in you? Who is ready to come out and play?

Does your home truly feel like "you" right now? Or is it an amalgam of someone else's style and ideas? *If you don't feel like yourself in your home, something needs to change.*

Are you struggling to define your personal style? Or do you know exactly what you want, all the time? *Either way, it's a good idea to visit museums, furniture shows, or open houses in your area to see what kinds of things resonate with you.*

Are you living with hand-me-downs that don't fit your sensibility? Do you wish you could throw everything away and start from scratch? *If you want to love what you have, you have to have things that you love. It is better to live with fewer things that you love passionately than a house full of disposable objects.*

Is your home like a hotel, with matched sets that feel too cookie-cutter? Do you ever wish that you had some more personal touches in your space? *The perfect furnishings don't always make for the perfect home. It's time to create a space that's rich with your soul's personal expression, with the depth of emotion that moves you and others who might experience your home.*

Is it a place you are proud to bring others to? Do you host dinner parties and other events? Or do you tend to avoid entertaining? *If you hesitate to bring people to your home, it's a sign that you don't think it really reflects you accurately, or that you don't want to be seen up close.*

What kind of clothing do you feel most like yourself in? *Is it relaxed yoga clothing or the business suit you wear to work? What does this tell you about the style of home that would best reflect the lifestyle you dream of?*

Using Your Things as a Mirror for Your Interior

Things aren't just physical objects — they are places where we house our deepest feelings and attachments. Our belongings can weigh us down, or they can make us feel buoyant. They can be attachments to difficult periods of our lives that we should be letting go of, or links to the most important parts of ourselves that we need to remember, respect, cherish, and bring back into the light.

As you walk from room to room, be aware of the emotions that come up in relation to the condition of your furniture and accessories and the memories attached to them. The necklace hanging on the mirror: was it given to you by the boyfriend who never gave you enough attention or by your beloved grandmother? Does it make you feel ignored and not quite good enough or confident and loved? Pay attention to what you do and do not feel attached to, and consider the reasons. Are they positive or negative? Do they elevate your mood or bring you down?

What is the first thing you see when you walk through the door? How does it make you feel? *When I enter my home, the first thing I see is a 400-year-old statue of Quan Yin, the Buddhist goddess of mercy. She reminds me of my desire to be a compassionate communicator, and every time I walk past her, subtly and unconsciously she communicates my greatest hope and wish for myself.*

Do your associations with your belongings lift you up or bring you down? *Analyzing the emotional components attached to your stuff can help you access your most blocked or hidden feelings.*

Do you have reminders of triumphs and successes placed where you can see them often? *Being proud of what you have accomplished leads to more accomplishments, if you remember to stay balanced. On the other hand, too much fixation on past successes can keep us from seeing the new paths that are open to us.*

What no longer reflects who you are now or where you see yourself in the future? *Sometimes things that have served us in the past are no longer useful as we continue to evolve into our more expanded selves.*

Is there a piece of yourself that you'd like to reclaim? *If there is a dream you'd like to honor, place a reminder front and center, whether it's a musical instrument, a piece of art that you created, or anything that makes you feel inspired or uplifted. Placing objects consciously in our space can remind us of our hopes and dreams and wishes for our lives as they quietly whisper to us.*

Is your home full of photographs of people? *Make sure you aren't looking into the faces of people who made you feel judged or incomplete; instead, surround yourself with photos of people who make you feel loved and cherished. Take a look at each picture and make sure you don't have any unresolved issues with anyone whose face you see every day.*

Are your closets, your drawers, and the space under your bed stuffed with old shoes, old photographs, and hidden resentments? *Consider each item and make sure you aren't hiding your incomplete emotions — or your valuable treasures, such as the photographs of the summer you spent volunteering in Africa that you've been meaning to frame forever — in these storage areas.*

Are there many items that you had forgotten about? Which of them do you miss having around? Which don't you need anymore?

If your home is new, have you made sure to display items that anchor you to the best parts of your past? *Maintaining a connection is important for balance.*

If you have been living in your home for years and years, have you made sure to include new things that represent who you are today? *Make room for the new and fuller you.*

Imagining Improvements

Home economics are a big source of concern for many people. Unfortunately, money is often a stand-in excuse for so many things that we avoid doing. Even when times are tough, we can keep our possessions clean and in good condition by polishing and dusting them regularly, showing how grateful we are for what we have.

We must trust in ourselves and in the world and not be afraid of throwing away old and broken things because we may not be able to replace them. If we have faith that we will be able to provide for ourselves, if we keep our eyes open for opportunity, everything we need will come our way. Create space, and trust that your life will expand to fill it. For now, just consider what improvements you can make, and take notes in a journal. You'll come back to these notes to readdress the improvements in later stages.

Making room for the new doesn't mean wasting. How can you adapt what you have and love so that it reflects your more evolved persona? What items can be repaired or improved? *Think about your chair that has a traditional skirt — what might it feel like if you got rid of the skirt and put wood legs on instead? What if you took the arm off your sofa and made it a chaise lounge?*

If you rent, what do you hesitate to improve since you don't own your home? *Brainstorm ways to turn your dreams into improvements or additions that you can bring with you, such as a piano instead of a recording studio, an easel instead of a kiln, or potted plants instead of an in-ground garden.*

If you own, what have you always meant to improve that you are finally ready to take the plunge on? *Do you want to install a Jacuzzi? Turn a porch into a screened-in family room? Replace carpets, refinish floors, put a window into a closed-up wall? How can you open your space so you can invite others in, or create areas for your own rejuvenation and relaxation?*

What would you love to change, even if you think you don't have the money? What changes have you been avoiding because of money? *Identifying desires, even if they're too big to take on right now, prepares the space to receive them later, when the time is right. Start a savings plan and work toward your goal so you can eventually make that change.*

What would you not give up if you had all the money in the world? *Living well isn't all about buying new things — it's also about appreciating what you already have. Deepening our connection to the things and people we love is part of living a more soulful life.*

MAKING SPACE FOR PASSIONATE LIVING

Nourishing your dreams will help you stay focused and happy, no matter who or what else demands your attention and care. Make room for your passions, and your passions will continue to ignite!

Can you indulge in your hobbies at home? Is there space to learn, to create, to wonder?

Are there rooms that are more like cubbyholes or storage areas than active places of enjoyment and living?

Is there a part of your home designated for having fun?

If you share your home with children or other adults, do you still have a private space that you can enjoy?

Room-by-Room Assessment

The following list of questions is designed to help you think about some of the practical concerns that often need to be addressed during a redesign. You'll want to modify this list for your needs and consider the questions thoughtfully and actively. When thinking about the living room, for instance, go and sit on the couch. Turn on the television. Invite your family to participate. You can also spread out your assessment over time and turn your awareness to how rooms and areas are used at family dinners and parties.

We'll be revisiting your room-by-room assessment in the CREATE chapter. For now, unpeel the layers of activity that take place in your home. Later, we'll use what you've gleaned to redesign your space and make it custom-fit to your lifestyle.

LIVING ROOM

- Who uses the room? Do children play here? Or do only adults use the room?
- Do you watch TV? Listen to music? Is the sound system adequate?
- Do you use it for hobbies or for leisure?
- Do you nap in the room?
- Do you read in the room? Is the lighting adequate?
- Do you entertain? How often? For a lot of people? Is there adequate seating?
- What else do you want to do in the room? What additions or changes can you make to support that activity?

DINING ROOM

- How often do you use your dining room? Daily? Weekly? Monthly? Only on special occasions?
- How many people usually eat at the dining room table?
- Is your table too large for everyday use? Is it large enough for special occasions and traditional celebrations?
- Is there enough room for someone to comfortably walk

around the table without people having to pull in their chairs?

- Is the height of the chairs comfortable for all members of the family?
- Is the room easily accessible from the kitchen and serving area?
- Do you have enough storage areas? Do you have enough serving areas?
- Is the lighting adequate?

KITCHEN

- What type of cook are you? How many people cook or help out at one time? Is the room big enough for everyone to move around comfortably without getting in each other's way?
- If your kitchen is used for entertaining, do you have sit-down meals or informal buffets?
- Do you have adequate storage for your canned and packaged foods and refrigerated and frozen foods? Your china, glassware, and cookware? Linens? Cookbooks? Wine?
- Are you happy with the height of your counters? Can you work for long periods without getting a backache?
- Can you reach the shelves in your cupboards without the use of a stepstool?
- Do you have an area set up for prep work by the sink? Are all your herbs, spices, oils, and so on set up conveniently by the stove?
- Do you have spot lighting by the stove and sink areas? Is the lighting adequate over the kitchen table? Do you have

good general lighting? Would under-cabinet lighting be helpful for doing your prep work?

BATHROOM(S)

- How many people use the bathroom regularly?
- Does it have to accommodate more than one person at a time during morning rush hour?
- Is there enough light?
- Is there enough mirror space?
- Are all faucets in good working order?
- Do you have enough hot water?
- Do you need more storage?
- Do you want to add fixtures? This could range from a new showerhead to a Jacuzzi bathtub.

BEDROOMS

- Is your bedroom the private, restful sanctuary you desire it to be?
- If you share the bedroom, is there sufficient room for two people to dress and move around comfortably?
- If you are looking for love, does your space reflect a romantic quality? Make sure your bed has room for more than one, and get rid of pictures of past lovers.
- Are you happy with the colors in your room? Do they make you feel peaceful and relaxed?
- Aside from sleeping, what do you do in your bedroom? Read, watch TV, talk on the telephone, work?
- If you put your makeup on in this room, is there a convenient spot with good lighting?

- Is the storage and closet space adequate for your clothing?
- Are guest rooms sanctuaries for visitors?

HOME OFFICE

- Do you work from home, or do you use your home office only occasionally?
- Do you have adequate and comfortable seating?
- Is the office a room of its own or does it do double duty as a guest bedroom or den?
- Do you have clients come to your home office? If so, is the entranceway professional and uncluttered?
- Is natural light adequate during the day? Do you need task lighting over your desk and work areas? Do you work nights and need brighter lights?
- Do you have adequate shelving and storage? Do you have adequate electrical outlets for lighting and all the necessary office equipment?

THE VIEW

When considering your rooms, do not forget about the outside views. The view you see influences how you feel; influencing the view can help you bring even more of what you need into your living space. In my bedroom, I have a bed that is on the same wall as a large picture window. I incorporated the window as if it were a part of the headboard, and outside I placed a large Buddha with beautiful palm trees, incorporating a sense of the sacred and the natural world.

My client Jennifer had a window in her very small living room that looked out on the backyard. The view was lovely, but it was the best thing about the room, which had room for a couch and that's about it. Just entering the space made her feel trapped, she told me, and so we took advantage of its best aspect — the view. We turned the large window into a pair of French doors, extending the space and creating an indoor and outdoor living room. This improved the flow, made the home feel larger, and took advantage of assets that were already present. By using ASSESS to see what she liked as well as what she didn't, we fixed the issues and made Jennifer feel more at home in her home. When assessing your rooms, pay attention to focal points, whether they are indoors or out!

- What can you see out your windows?
- How could changing what you see outside enhance the space inside?

The active contemplation, investigation, and honesty with yourself that you've employed in your assessment will provide the information and tools you need to move through the next stages. As in a video game, you can't get to the next level without successfully navigating the stage you are in. In Stage 2, RELEASE, you will let go of the belongings that you began to realize no longer served you when you assessed. In Stage 3, CLEANSE, you will clean and polish the things that you have learned support the person you are as much as the person you are becoming. DREAM, DISCOVER, CREATE, ELEVATE, and CELEBRATE all tie into the revitalized self-understanding you've gained during ASSESS.

EXERCISE: WRITE A POST-ASSESSMENT LOVE LETTER

Pick one item that you absolutely love and that has really spoken to you during your assessment. Write a letter to it. Tell it how you feel, why you appreciate it, and why you couldn't live without it.

As you move through the rest of the stages, remember this item and why you chose it. The thing that you feel the most connected to can be the starting point for the design of your entire home. For example, I have a crystal-and-copper staff that I find especially gorgeous. The colors, the texture, and the shape not only are aesthetically pleasing but also speak to me on a deeper level, reminding me of my most sacred self. When I remodeled my home, I called the staff to mind again and again as an example of the way I wanted my home to feel.

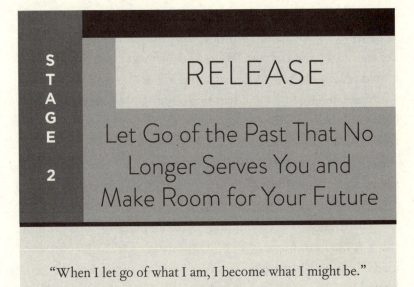

RELEASE

Let Go of the Past That No Longer Serves You and Make Room for Your Future

"When I let go of what I am, I become what I might be."

— LAO TZU

etting go can be hard. It can be *really* hard. It takes a lot of courage, all our residual hope, and all the good feelings and positive spirits we can muster. Do you remember Marsha, the divorced woman who could not let go of her wedding gown? It initially seemed as if my assessment with Marsha had ended in... nothing. A week went by, and then two, and I wanted to call her; I didn't because I knew that it was up to her to decide to make a change in her life.

Nearly five months later, Marsha finally called. When she said her name on the phone, it took me a minute to remember her. "From art class?" she said. I didn't get it. "With the wedding dress?" Now I knew who she was. She asked if I would meet her for lunch, and I agreed. Who could have guessed that Marsha would practically weep into her Greek salad?

She explained that she had put on the dress, and instead of being imbued with the wonderful memories and happy, hopeful feelings she had experienced wearing the gown at her wedding, she felt anxious and concerned, angry and upset. "It fit perfectly," she told me. "And I just didn't feel like myself in it. I started crying before I had even zipped it up."

The dress had been holding her raw emotions for her until she was ready to process them. Until the day when Marsha was ready to truly face these emotions and finish letting go of the pain, it was just hanging there in the closet, waiting for her to be ready. If we have unfinished business, our souls will not let us get away with not completing and releasing these emotions. We unconsciously create and manifest things and objects in our lives and in our homes that act as placeholders for these emotions. When we are ready, we can confront and begin to work through them, using the physical objects as tools for growth.

In order to grow, Marsha brought the dress to her local Salvation Army and donated it so that another bride could have the opportunity to feel beautiful in that dress and she could complete the process of letting go of the pain in her past so she could embrace a brighter future.

Catharsis Is Never Easy

For Marsha, getting rid of the dress became an emotional experience that helped her let go, even though she hadn't known that she was holding on. It took less time for her to decide to sign the divorce papers than to get rid of that dress! By releasing the object that tied her to a relationship that no longer served her, she released her fears that every relationship would ultimately end in the same way.

"I feel more comfortable now," she said, "with myself, with my life."

"Why do you think that is?" I asked.

"I can look in my closet now without a big white reminder that things can go wrong. That isn't how I want to see the world anymore."

"And?" I said. I had noticed that she was wearing her hair in a different style, and a much brighter lipstick than I remembered.

"And I just started dating someone," she said. "Just a few weeks ago. I don't know what's going to happen...and I feel very happy."

Now it was I who was almost crying into my greens. I was overwhelmed with appreciation for Marsha's struggle, and for her persistence. Letting go is hard! Remember that. And it is always worth it. Just on the other side of pain is freedom.

Every day and every week, I am amazed at the things that come my way — when I get out of my own way. The universe wants to give us so much. It is ripe with so much joy and so much abundance. Yet we close our eyes to possibilities, drowning out the whispers of hope in favor of hanging on to what is old and familiar. Once we identify the blocks and clear the pathways in our own homes, we can clear the pathways to our buried emotions. When the floodgates open and the pain is allowed to be released, our dreams and hopes begin to pour through.

Releasing the belongings that carry painful memories will remind you that you are in control and that you shape your surroundings and your destiny. Letting go frees you, physically and metaphysically, creating space for the new you and your bright future to shine.

Making Room for the Future

Michele first got in touch with me because she wanted to explore ways to make over the cottage where she and her teenage daughter lived. She was dealing with a lot of recent changes — none of which she had wanted. Her husband had left her, and nobody had asked her how she felt about being a single mom. And her child, who she wished was still a little girl, was a teenager, with her own life and her own agenda. Michele was stuck in the past, a time when she was carefree and her baby was still a baby. Things had changed, and she had to catch up, fast.

Sometimes we make conscious decisions to change our lives. More often, our lives change before we think we are ready. We lose a job. A loved one passes away. A relationship ends or changes, or a child grows up. And we cling to the past, when things felt "normal" and we didn't have to bend with the wind. It is imperative that we really live where we are, that we see the world accurately, so we can best take advantage of the particular opportunities inherent in each moment. Change is a normal part of living. Everything changes.

The more we become comfortable with change, the easier life becomes. Embrace change, and you are really embracing life. Making room for change allows you to see the beauty and the love that are always around you.

This was the challenge for Michele, as I learned soon after we started working together. When I met her and her daughter, Sara, they were stuck in limbo between the old and the new. The two lived in a tiny cottage with a ton of character; as is often the case, there was a lot more going on in this home beneath the surface. I saw it immediately upon approaching the walkway leading to the back property. The house numbers mounted on the gate were missing one digit, and the mailbox was broken and obscured, barely visible from the street.

Aside from obvious issues of safety, I thought about how our address and our mailbox are prime ways that people and the universe use to find us. How can the universe grant us our wishes if nobody knows where we live?

How would friends find her house for a party? By looking at the addresses on the houses on either side? What about emergencies? What about serendipity? It would definitely be a challenge for the universe to provide for the inhabitants of the home if even the post office couldn't find them because their address was incomplete!

The outside of their home could have been adorable if it hadn't been in such shabby condition. The fence was falling down, which gave me a clue that there were boundary issues in this home. And the yard, which Michele called the secret garden, was just dirt and a bunch of weeds, not a daisy or a lilac in sight.

As we walked through the house, I could see that she had collected an amazing number of sacred objects, including one that had been given to her by the Dalai Lama. They were all just thrown around as if they were clutter, as if she didn't care about them. As I asked her to talk about everything around us, Michele saw her place with fresh eyes.

During this real look at the property, Michele was surprised to see that the address number was missing, although she walked by it every day and it would be a relatively easy thing to fix. As we made our way to the front door we talked about the fact that the fence dividing the main house from the cottage was practically toppled over on its side. It seemed as if Michele was living unconsciously in her home and unaware of what she was out of contact with; she was not taking any responsibility for what was manifesting itself in her space. As she shifted into a more conscious awareness, this new, raw and unfiltered point of view helped her begin to connect all her emotional baggage with the many physical cues of neglect: the missing address number, the falling fence, the messiness of the space. It was obvious from her negligence of the place that she wished she was someplace else, or perhaps nowhere at all. But this was where she was, and this was where her life had taken her, and she needed to come face-to-face with that fact and care for herself and her daughter now, today. Acceptance is the key to true change.

As I got to know Michele and her space, it became apparent how important it was for her to be a good mother and provide for her daughter in a manner that she herself had not been afforded while growing up. She spoke with great pride about Sara's numerous accomplishments and was happy to show me the various awards and certificates on display. Clearly, she didn't view her own professional accomplishments as worthy of being put out for others to see.

The living room walls were adorned with cartoon art, movie memorabilia, and caricatural sketches of mother and daughter. The photos on the mantel were of Sara as a baby, a child, and a teenager — the only photos of Michele showed her as a teenager. In fact, the entire cottage spoke of two teenage girls. Michele expressed herself in her home not as a professional, able adult but as a rebellious teenager still struggling to find herself.

I made a mental note of this, and then we moved on to the bedrooms. A bedroom is, naturally, a very intimate part of one's home. Because only very close family or friends will be in those spaces, many people put less care into the appearance of their bedrooms. And so bedrooms can sometimes speak volumes — much more than, say, a porch or a dining room.

Sara's bedroom looked like what you would expect for a teenage girl: stuffed with clothes, posters, and knickknacks. Still, it was relatively clean, the cleanest room in the house and the most well organized. I was impressed, until Michele confessed that Sara didn't sleep in the room, preferring to spend her nights in her mom's room and using her own room essentially as a dressing room and study space.

I thought immediately of the knocked-down fence outside. Here was another clear example of a boundary being ignored. Why was a teenager sleeping with her mother? I wondered about this even more when I saw Michele's room, which was a horror show.

Clothes were strewn about. A witch marionette hung over the bed, looming over the space and adding a very creepy touch to the unkempt room. Also, a possessed-looking doll, which Michele told me had "real human hair," sat on a dresser in the corner.

Michele joked about not having many male visitors, and it was clear that this bothered her. It was just as clear that she had created barriers that might prevent any intimacy, other than that which she shared with her daughter, from entering her home.

What we had here was a child who was growing up and still stuck to her mother. Sara was bright and accomplished, and she needed to live in her own room in preparation for living in her own apartment when she became an adult, a time that was not far off. We also had a mother who was still trying to figure out how to be a grown-up. From the falling-down fencing to the home's dormlike atmosphere, this family needed to make some changes.

Michele and Sara needed to make shifts in their home so they could move forward on their journey together as a family, and on their own personal journeys as women. Michele had to connect with herself as a single adult instead of acting like a child. Sara, first and foremost, needed to sleep in her own room.

We retired to the kitchen to talk this out, and I noticed wooden letters that spelled out B-O-Y-S hanging on the wall. When I asked Michele and Sara who they belonged to, Michele said they were hers. "After all," she continued, "don't we all love boys?" With that, she winked at me. I was taken aback, and I gently told her that I was in a relationship with a man, not a boy.

Michele was very resistant to changing her style. She believed that her youthful accoutrements were the source of her creativity and flair. After a lot of consideration she began to let go of her attachments to her inner teenager and removed some of the items in the home that didn't appropriately reflect her role as a parent — such as the wooden letters, which went right into the trash. Along with the letters, she also released the puppet of the witch that was hanging over her bed — and scaring off all the men she ever brought home — and the doll that was sitting on her dresser. All these things were pushing men and intimacy away. Michelle and Sara also had to put away all the drawings that Sara had done years before and close the door on the younger child, as her daughter was becoming a young woman. Sara went back to sleeping in her own bed.

During the RELEASE phase it is important to connect to the things that you are releasing. Michelle needed to connect to the emotions tied to the things she was holding on to. If we don't uncover why we have been holding on to certain objects, those emotions will remain unresolved, and before long we'll just accumulate more objects to hold the unresolved issues and emotions.

Our DREAM, DISCOVER, and CREATE stages focused on

creating a family home with distinct and appropriate sleeping areas and a shared space that could be used for eating and reading. Michele ended up moving most of the Sara-focused items out of the living room and re-creating the living space. We gathered all her scattered sacred objects — beads from India, stones from her travels through Tibet, and a scarf that had been blessed by the Dalai Lama. We hung the beads on the wall, centered a Buddha statue beneath them, and draped the statue with the scarf. We organized the rocks from Tibet around the statue, and nearby we hung a beautiful picture of a guru with whom Michele had shared a profound experience. By pulling her belongings out of the corners and gathering them together, we were able to focus their energy. Now when Michele walks through her living room, something she does unconsciously multiple times a day, she is reminded of her sacred self, who she truly is on the inside — not a person with little control over her own life but an individual with strong values and beliefs. RELEASE was exactly what Michele needed: to let go of the childish toys and associations and reclaim the objects that spoke to her maturity, her wisdom, and her experience.

No matter what you love, whether it is cooking, art, music, or poetry, let it out. Show it. Display it. Wear your heart on your sleeve! Cooks can display their antique cookbooks, their fine collection of esoteric French cooking tools, their recently sprouted globe basil. Enthusiasts can frame and display their most prized stamps or mount their ukulele collection, their sports trophies, or their medals of valor. Are you proud of your education? Hang your diploma. Was your business mentioned in a local paper? Frame the article. Are you a budding Buddhist? Create an altar, as Michele did. When you surround yourself with tokens of your passions, your inner self can become your external world, and your external world can then reinforce your inner self.

More Is Less. Even More Is Unthinkable.

If you were on a sinking ship, what is the first thing you would do? You'd probably get rid of the extra weight. It's amazing how many of us are living in "sinking ships," lives that require too much of our energy and don't give us enough in return, and we think that the answer is to acquire more instead of having less. Clutter is making us crazy, and not just because we can't find anything — because every bit of wood, metal, and plastic we collect is an anchor tying us to something, somebody, somewhere.

You know your neighbors who have two-car garages? Twenty-five percent of them are parking at least one car outside — the U.S. Department of Energy says they have so much extra stuff there's not enough room in the garage for the second car! More facts: Getting rid of clutter would eliminate 40 percent of housework in the average home. One out of eleven families in the United States rents a space to store their extra junk, wasting about $1,000 a year in the process. All that junk is costing us valuable time and money, not to mention a heap of unnecessary emotional attachments.

So why can't we let it go?

Doesn't having fewer, more cherished belongings that really inspire you sound a whole lot better than just coping with the side effects of living with so much extra stuff? This false sense of abundance isn't buoying us up — it's sinking us.

The Browns

I hadn't realized how extreme the clutter issue could get until I met the Brown family through one of the employees at my company. Their story was a sad one, filled with missed opportunities and unfulfilled expectations. Richard and Evelyn Brown were coming up on forty years of marriage and contemplating a divorce. Their inability to "get it together" throughout their lives had brought them to a place where they were subsisting on food stamps and living in government-subsidized housing. They were both depressed, morbidly overweight, and suffering serious health issues. In their sunset years, when they should have been enjoying retirement in the home they had created and made their own, they were worrying about whether to pay for groceries or medicine.

Before I met Richard and Evelyn, I spent some time with their daughter, Teresa. Teresa was smart, thoughtful, and attractive but, like her parents, not financially "successful" or even financially stable. Over coffee, she talked about her family, sharing with me the painful details of her upbringing. I expected her to mention lost opportunities because of their financial situation, but the picture that emerged was even more shocking. Her mother, she explained, was a classic hoarder. As a child, Teresa had avoided having friends over for fear that she would have to clear pathways for them through the accumulated clutter and debris in her home.

"Everything was saved," she said to me, her voice ringing with desperation. "Leftovers. Newspapers. Junk mail. Broken furniture. Everything that came into our home stayed there."

Teresa still carried a lot of anger toward her mother and father. When I later saw her interacting with them, all her words toward them blistered with recrimination and contempt for who they were and what they had done to her. The entire family was still tortured by the past and unable to move forward into a brighter future.

Teresa and I agreed to go look at the storage spaces the family was renting, for not inconsiderable expense. Even with the knowledge that Teresa's mom was a hoarder, I was not remotely prepared for what I discovered. Twenty-year-old canned goods. Over a thousand ketchup packets. Magazines and takeout menus and empty cat food containers. Teresa was ready to throw everything away — her painful childhood, her bad memories. Once we got rid of what was clearly junk — and a health risk — we started to peel back the layers of the lives that Evelyn and Richard had lived. She had once been an actress, slim and lovely. He had been a commander in the British Navy. This elderly couple, calcified by years of regret and self-loathing, had actually led pretty remarkable lives. As I observed Teresa taking it all in, I suggested that we stop our work and regroup the following day.

I intuitively knew that Teresa's parents had to be a part of this process, so I contacted them and brought them to the storage unit the next day. When we showed up, Teresa was shocked to see that her parents were in the van with me. However, despite her initial misgivings, the next few hours were magical. The family came alive as they shared memories connected with their things — the old family room TV that played only four channels, the church organ that had filled their apartment with music when Richard would play on the weekends, and so on. We found a commendation from the Queen of England that had been awarded to Richard and a certificate for a Hollywood Star of Tomorrow that Evelyn had received early in her acting career. Teresa was getting to see a different side of her parents, as hopeful, successful people, and I could see the energy shift. She had been ready to throw everything out; now she saw the objects in storage as holding the cellular memory of her family.

We cleared out the four storage spaces and consolidated everything into one unit. In reconnecting with the items they had hidden away, Evelyn and Richard rediscovered their joy and felt more comfortable donating many of their items to charities so the items could make their way to new homes and be used once again. This process of RELEASE allowed the positive memories to find their place in the sun, unobstructed by years and years of emotional debris. And in the next phase, CLEANSE, Teresa took a few mementos, polished and shined them, and placed them prominently in her home as a way to honor the best of her parents.

The RELEASE process renewed the Browns' affection and familial bonds. The love had always been there; it was just buried under a mountain of inconsequential objects that were obstructing a clear view to what was really important and worth holding on to.

Rinse, Repeat

Most of us, while we hold on to parts of the past that we no longer need, are not as extreme in our attachments as the Browns were. However, too often we take our cues for how to live today from the way we lived yesterday, when the right thing to do is to create entirely new patterns based on intention and introspection.

Lia was referred to me by another client. She and her daughter, Ella, were about to move into a new apartment after Lia's painful split from Michael, Ella's dad. At our first consultation, Lia was conflicted. She told me she was furious with Michael for having cheated on her and for never having been around because he was at work. He had been closer to his work than to his family, she lamented. However, she realized that Michael was a good father even though he was a terrible husband. So when it was time to clean out their old home, her first instinct was to throw in the trash everything that bore Michael's impression and completely erase the memory of him. On the other hand, it was important to her that Ella have a healthy relationship with her father that wasn't tainted by the fact that Lia and Michael were no longer together, so she wasn't sure how to proceed.

When life changes in such a significant way, whether because of a divorce, a new job, or a new relationship, it's important to look at your living space again and move things out and around. If Lia hadn't had a child, I might have agreed with her initial instinct; in this case, I knew her RELEASE would have to come in a different way. After all, if she was trying to get rid of every reminder of her ex, she was going to have a tough time of it — Ella was the spitting image of her dad, with big blue eyes and curly dark hair, just like the man I saw in the photos Lia wanted to toss.

As we talked, my eyes strayed to the items she had placed in the "keep" section. I noticed a bunch of toys and stuffed animals in a clear protective case.

"Were those Ella's?" I asked.

"No," she said. "They were mine. My dad got them for me." I imagined a picture-perfect childhood. Lia quickly corrected me. She said she had grown up in a single-parent home from the time she was three years old. Her father's absence had defined a lot of her childhood memories. He would promise to be there for holidays, recitals, and other milestone events, and when the time came he would be a no-show. There would always be some excuse and a material token of apology with promises to "do better next time."

"It looks like every one of those toys represents an apology," I said.

"Yeah, but this didn't," said Lia, pointing to a delicate chain necklace with a lovely cameo, which hung in her jewelry case. "It was my grandmother's," she said. "My father gave it to me when Ella was born."

As an adult Lia had promised herself that she would never marry a man like her father. And when she met Michael, he seemed to be exactly what she'd been looking for. He owned his home, he had been at the same job for a decade, and he seemed like the essence of stability. They were married shortly after they met, and Lia settled into a life of domesticity while focusing on her career as a magazine writer.

Over the next few years, however, conflict arose. Michael's job as an executive at a multinational corporation led to fairly regular relocation when he was asked to open up new markets for his company. The constant moving started to wear on Lia, who had to try to make new friends in a different city every couple of years, and created a rift in her marriage.

After Ella was born, they moved to Los Angeles, where things seemed a bit more stable...until Lia discovered that Michael was having an affair. When Michael's company decided to move him again, Lia decided that she had had enough. And since he had already cheated on her, she was not going to trust him living in a different city for a while. They needed to stay in one place, and Michael refused: he wanted to go. After ten years of marriage, Lia and Michael divorced. He moved and left her with the responsibility of selling their LA-area home. They agreed that Ella would stay with her mother during the school year and spend vacations and summers with her father.

I realized that before Lia could begin to deal with her feelings for Michael, she needed to confront her feelings about her father. He had passed away, so there was no way for her to connect with him directly. What she *could* do was choose what memories of him she would keep and cherish. We agreed that she would let the stuffed animals go, since they represented her childhood feelings of abandonment, and keep the necklace, which tied her to her grandmother and was a wonderful example of her father's presenting her with a very thoughtful gift that was not an apology but was a token of love and congratulations.

Lia cried when we moved the case of toys into the "toss" pile. I knew this was enough for one day, and after a big hug, I left her to manage her move and record her feelings in her journal.

A few weeks later, when I came to her new home to help her plan and organize the space, she answered the door looking very peaceful, with the gold cameo hanging around her neck. As we moved through the sparsely furnished living room, taking stock of what she wanted and needed to add to make this home a happy one for her daughter, I was pleased to see photos of Ella and her dad framed beautifully around the apartment. I also noticed a black-and-white snapshot of a very little girl holding the hand of a handsome young man.

"Who is that?" I asked, even though I thought I knew.

"Me and my father," said Lia with a smile, as her hand strayed up to her necklace.

Little Things Can Mean a Lot

In my own life, I have actively cultivated the SoulSpace mind-set and find myself constantly assessing, releasing, cleansing, and so on. But even I become stuck in my attachments, sometimes clinging to objects that I think represent freedom when in fact they represent the chains that fetter me to my past.

For a number of years, I have been in a loving, wonderful relationship with Jason, an amazing and talented man who helps me see the joy that can be found every single day. Before I was lucky enough to meet Jason, I was stuck in a relationship that wasn't only unfulfilling — it was actually hurting me. I ended that relationship with a bruised and heavy heart, and I thought I had moved forward — except I did not find myself connecting with anyone new. I went on dates, I met people, and...nothing. No sparks. No feeling of connection, of truly knowing somebody new as if I had known him for a thousand years.

I knew I had to reassess the way I was living and see what clues where hiding in my home. I assessed and could not see what the problem was. I walked around seeing what things I could release, and nothing major jumped out at me. While digging through a closet in my family room, I discovered a photograph of my old lover. It was a candid snapshot I had taken during a vacation — a small image, something that seemed entirely inconsequential. This photo was still in its frame and hidden in the closet. Sometimes the things that are the most hidden hold the most energy to release!

Suddenly, it was as if my whole being was on fire. This was it. It wasn't the very large sofa in the living room; it wasn't the wrought-iron table in the dining room. It was this little, hidden photo that was the glaring clue: I needed to release my old relationship in order to cultivate the mindfulness and appreciation of myself that would allow me to find someone special.

I created a special moment: I spoke some words of forgiveness, for him and for myself for holding on for all these years. I felt some emotions of the loss...and released the memory and photo through a burning ceremony I created. I also wrote about my feelings of disappointment in my journal so that I could release myself and create the space to receive someone new. As I burned the photograph, watching the edges wilt and melt and the image disappear into the fire, I could feel all my regrets and frustrations melting away.

Believe it or not, soon after this RELEASE I met Jason, the man who was and is the light of my life!

Separating the Wheat from the Chaff

What did you notice during your ASSESS stage that just doesn't belong anymore? Room by room, collect and release the extra weight, and set yourself free. At the start of this journey, think about whether it would be easier to have someone with you. Having a good friend support you in the process can bring some clarity, assist you in overcoming resistance to releasing things, and support you in working through the emotions that come up.

Consider each object in your home. If you're not sure whether to release it, use the following guidelines to help you decide.

If you do not absolutely love it, release it.

If it does not make you feel amazing, get rid of it.

If it is beautiful but it makes you feel lousy, let it go.

If it is broken and beyond repair, toss it.

If it is expensive and carries negative emotional weight, sell it.

If it is in good condition and no longer feels like yours, donate it.

If you find yourself resisting letting go of certain items, don't fall into the trap of simply putting them into storage. Garages, basements, and attics are full of items that should have been released but instead continue to collect dust and, more important, weigh on their owners emotionally.

Create a "keep" pile for the things you want to keep and a

"toss" pile for the things you want to let go of. Then donate, sell, or recycle everything you can, and trash the rest.

Deciding whether to release furniture, personal photographs, and artwork can be tricky. I've provided the following pointers to help you. You considered many of these questions in ASSESS, so keep in mind the insights you uncovered in that stage. Now is the time to act on some of them by deciding to release what isn't working.

FURNITURE

Look over each piece of furniture carefully. Consider the architectural peculiarities of your home at the same time. My living room in Los Angeles has angled walls instead of traditional 90-degree corners. Before I renovated, I thought about the couches I had: there was something about them that felt wrong, that clashed with my appreciation of the individuality of the space. When I renovated, I used the information I had gathered in my assessment to release those couches, giving them to a friend who had always loved them. Instead of cursing those angled walls for making furniture shopping awkward, I decided to really embrace the angles and incorporate them into my new furniture choices. Now I have two sofas floating in the middle of the living room — and the backs of the sofas have the same angles as the walls.

When you're taking a fresh look at your furniture, I'd like you to consider it on three levels:

- The emotional. If you have a chair that is beautiful but was an inheritance from a horrid old aunt who always made you feel terrible about yourself, let it go. Beauty that makes you feel bad should not be in your home.
- The practical. What is just taking up space? What is

creating clutter instead of creating comfort? How comfortable is the furniture? Do you actually use it? If there is a table that is never used or a chair that nobody sits in, why is it there? Focus on functionality, not your sentimental attachments. If you love something but it is in disrepair, fix it or let it go!

- The aesthetic. Look at the furniture you've had for ages that you don't think much about: now is your chance to identify the pieces that no longer suit you. What doesn't fit the way you live? The way you dress? The way you see yourself? What looks shabby or outmoded?

Following are a few more ways to examine your furniture.

- Look at the colors. What pieces are the color you'd like to re-create in your new home? What pieces are jarring because of the color and just don't fit anymore? Can they be reupholstered? If not, let them go.
- Feel the texture. Is the furniture nice to touch as well as see? If there is a possibility of splinters, let it go. If the couch is too scratchy to sit on in shorts, let it go.
- Consider the proportions. Do things feel too big for the space or too small? Are pieces of furniture blocking entrances or passageways? Is there too much furniture or too little? Too much means that eliminating a few pieces will open the space. Too little furniture makes a room feel unused and bare — cavernous or neglected instead of cozy and cared for.

Photographs of Friends and Family

During RELEASE, consider each image in your home. Does it remind you of good times? Does it remind you of a person who loved and supported you? Does it connect you to the best parts of your past? If not, release it.

ART

When we have art for a long time, we can stop really seeing it. Not every wall needs to be adorned! Make sure your art is still resonant and special to you; otherwise, pass it on to someone who will appreciate it more than you do. Release it!

As you look once more at everything in your home, with the things you noticed during ASSESS fresh in your mind, think about whether each item inspires you or is just taking up space. You no longer have time for things or situations or people that just inhabit your space without contributing! Release those things! Once you start to let go in your home, you will unconsciously start doing the same thing in all the other areas of your life. The SoulSpace process starts at home and then from that center reverberates throughout your life.

EXERCISE: WRITE A GOOD-BYE LETTER

Which object did you most need to release? What was the hardest or the most satisfying — or both! — to let go of? Write a letter to it. Tell it how you feel, why you appreciated it in the past, why it no longer serves you, and why you are letting it go.

By connecting to the emotions you are releasing along with the object, you will help yourself truly be free.

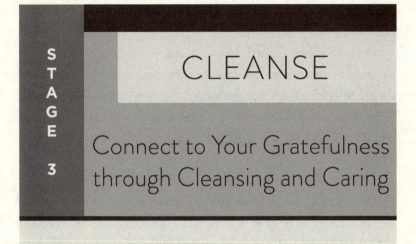

CLEANSE

Connect to Your Gratefulness through Cleansing and Caring

> "If a man's mind becomes pure,
> his surroundings will also become pure."
>
> — BUDDHA

While the above quotation from the Buddha is true, the reverse is also true: if we make our surroundings pure, our minds become pure in the process, and that which was obscured from view can be held up to the light to shine.

When I met my client Larry, a gifted photographer, he was lonely, stuck in the past, and struggling financially. As we moved around his home during the initial assessment, he kept making excuses for the fact that he couldn't seem to pick up any new clients. "I haven't been so into photography lately," he said first. Later he mentioned the tough competition, the picky clients, and the rough market as reasons why he wasn't doing as well as he had been a few years prior.

As we walked around, I noticed that while he was in his early forties, his apartment looked as if someone much younger lived there. Instead of framed paintings, posters covered the walls. Instead of a work area, his kitchen table was heaped with files and Post-its. There was a pile of dust under the table, along with a fork.

This was not the space of a professional adult.

You would never have guessed that for the majority of his career, Larry had been in high demand, focusing mostly on celebrity photography. When magazines needed someone to send on an important shoot, Larry had been the person they called. He had also had a partner for ten years, a relationship that had ended about two years before I met him. A resulting feeling of loss still hovered around his apartment — upon entering his home, I sensed a heavy, sad feeling that permeated every corner of the space. Since the loss of that relationship, his career had slowed to a stop.

Larry's apartment was in shambles; it looked like a storage facility. Larry's stuff included junk that needed to be released as well as items that needed to be cleansed and cherished. Past the piles of paper and the tins from last night's takeout dinner, scattered amid the junk, in different drawers and closets, were the cameras he had used in the various phases of his career. There was one from his days as a young student of photography that was fully manual, one from his early career as a young journalist, and a whole bunch of extralong lenses from his years as a celebrity photographer.

Then, as we worked to release the useless piles that were cluttering up his kitchen workspace, and his psyche, we made a very important discovery. In a file cabinet that was jammed full of papers, we found some incredible celebrity photos that Larry had taken. Instead of displaying them proudly, showing himself and the world what he had accomplished, he had hidden his successes away — and this tendency was being reflected in his stagnant career. His passions and his successes were literally hidden beneath the clutter of his present life, and this was keeping him from the successful future he so desperately wanted.

As part of Larry's CLEANSE phase, we got rid of every piece of junk mail that was littering his apartment, cleaned all the dirt out of the corners, and caught all those dust bunnies and banished them. Along with the dirt and dust bunnies went the depressive feeling that had been hovering in the apartment.

We cleaned out the clutter that was obstructing Larry's view of who he was. We made piles. We cleaned every inch of the apartment. We gave Larry a fresh new start.

Most important, we reclaimed his past success by framing his celebrity photographs and placing them around his home in prominent places. By seeing these photos, Larry could be reminded every day that he was a very creative man who had hit a rough patch, not a talentless hack who needed to find a new career. Each image was a reminder that he could do it — and would do it again.

We also collected all the old cameras and created an artistic display. By seeing this daily, Larry would be reminded that he loved to take pictures, and of all the stages that had brought him to where he was.

With this kind of subtle daily encouragement, his attitude began to shift. His actions changed. Instead of waiting for success to land in his lap, he went after new clients more aggressively. He felt more confident and more professional, and he acted it. He began to invite agents over for dinner, and they introduced him to their clients in turn. Once the stars and starlets got wind of the new Larry, he started to get lucrative freelance work.

Larry was shocked, and I wasn't surprised in the least. I've seen it happen time and time again. Finding your dreams, shining them carefully, and letting them live in the light helps make them a reality.

Spring-Cleaning for the Soul

The CLEANSE phase comprises the key actions of literally cleansing and caring for cherished belongings, and performing metaphysical cleansing rituals that help us emotionally and energetically clear our spaces. In the previous stage, we talked about how beneficial it can be to let go. In CLEANSE, which counterbalances RELEASE, we learn how to reconnect with our valued possessions via simple-seeming activities such as dusting, washing, framing, and reupholstering. By getting rid of the unnecessary extras in RELEASE, we make room to acquire new belongings and to honor the ones we actively choose to keep. We do this by caring for them anew in CLEANSE.

Cleansing is an important ritual of care and preparation. The idea is to breathe new life into existing items and space. Cleansing polishes the outer world and lets the inner self shine; it is a way of nurturing and caring for yourself. In the previous stage, you worked to rid yourself of emotional cobwebs. Now you will reconnect with the belongings that make you feel inspired and loved. As you renew your bonds to what is useful for you, you strengthen your connection to the parts of your history that are the foundation of who you are today and who you want to become.

Cleanse in Order to Connect

Many of my clients feel closely rooted to their family histories, and that includes the belongings that are passed from generation to generation with care and love. When these heirlooms are properly handled and cared for and given prominence in the home, they represent a beautiful "passing of the torch" that honors the past while rooting it in the present. Unfortunately, a lot of people hold on to things that were passed along because they're unable to let go of emotions and unresolved feelings in their family. These people need to go back and reread the chapter on RELEASE!

In these cases, the heirlooms become artifacts, better suited for a museum than a home. This was certainly true of my client Cristina. She and her husband, Dave, were newly married and living in a rented home in the suburbs. They were adamant about wanting to work with me, bubbling over with excitement about their idea of turning an unused den into a recording studio they could both share. A fascinating pair, they are the perfect embodiment of "opposites attract," and they make their partnership work through laughter and a shared passion for the arts. This was clear as soon as I met them at a party given by a mutual friend, with Dave making loud jokes about all the children they were going to have, and Cristina vigorously shaking her head at me every time he turned around.

This was quite a funny show; it had the added effect of demonstrating Dave's excitement about an area of their lives that Cristina was either afraid of or disinclined toward. When I got to their house he immediately began this line of joking, and she responded with head shaking again; it was clear this was a routine they had worked out, and I wondered what it all really meant. My attention to this "to have or not to have children" banter was distracted as soon as we entered their shared living space.

The homes of creative, busy people often reflect the busy quality of their daily lives. When everyone is caught up in the creative fire, things like dusting can fall through the cracks. So I often expect to see a bit of chaos when entering the home of somebody whose artistic passion I am acquainted with. In this case, *chaos* doesn't adequately describe what I found. It was not a clutter of books and music and art; it was a dingy space with papers piled high, dusty counters, and a staleness in the air that completely overwhelmed my senses.

The living room was teeming with dusty and disheveled furniture and dishes that Cristina said "belonged to grandma." In her mind, having these things honored the memory of a woman who had played an important role in her life and early childhood development. Unfortunately, neglecting instead of properly maintaining these items and keeping them clean seemed to represent instability instead of the stability that was her intention.

Before we could get to the DREAM, DISCOVER, and CREATE stages, we had to deal with the ancient mess in the main shared space. Cristina clearly loved her grandmother, who had been her primary caregiver and, in her mind, the only person who had believed in her before she met her husband. Her parents were a different story altogether. They had not believed in her or given her a strong belief in herself; it was only because of her grandmother's love that she had flourished into the strong woman who was standing before me.

She became very upset whenever her parents were mentioned, and I wondered how connected this was to the way she deflected the subject of kids whenever it came up.

What Cristina needed was not a RELEASE, which would have separated her from her grandmother, but a CLEANSE that would enable her to see, hold, and connect to her heirlooms while making them her own via the process of physically cleaning them.

As we dusted and washed all the heirlooms, from beautiful china with a delicate rose pattern and 18-karat gold inlay to an umbrella stand with a big crack in it, Cristina shared story after story about her grandmother. "I cracked that umbrella stand," she admitted. "I was so scared to tell my grandma. But then all she did was glue it and turn it around so the crack didn't show. When I see it now, it brings up so many memories."

I left her and Dave to talk about this. I had a hunch that this flood of emotion had a source that was contemporary instead of from yesteryear.

When I came back for our next consultation, the living room was sparkling, and the musty smell had been replaced by the delicate scent of jasmine flowers. They had also made great headway in clearing out the den, which was to be the new recording studio.

"We have another idea," said Cristina. She sounded almost shy.

"Idea for what?" I said, watching them look at each other as if they were daring each other to say it first.

"For the den," she said, "instead of a recording studio. Which we still want. Which can go upstairs."

"For what?" I asked again, getting the feeling that this was going to be an important answer.

"For a nursery," said Dave, practically bursting. "A huge nursery! With room for five!"

"A small nursery," said Cristina. "To start."

The simple act of cleaning reintroduced Cristina to a relationship she had relegated to history. With the loss of her grandmother, she had felt disconnected from the loving family relationship she had been lucky enough to experience as a little girl. By holding each of her grandmother's possessions, by remembering the stories it held, she was able to realize that despite her mother's inability to give her the affection she needed, she could emulate her grandmother and give her own children a magical childhood of acceptance and nurturing. She had finally realized that she could model her attitudes as a mother after her grandmother, who had loved and cherished her, instead of her neglectful mother. It was her negative connection to her *parents* that she worked to release. Her *grandmother*, on the other hand, was an ideal icon for her to emulate.

Cleansing across Continents and Cultures

Around the world and across the centuries, people have recognized the powers of cleaning for hygiene and dust control, for ritualizing seasonal changes, and for metaphysical cleansing, meant to rid a home of spirits and negative energy as much as cobwebs — from the Catholic tradition of using holy water to purify spaces to Native American and Middle Eastern rituals to the rigorous cleaning of the home before Tibetan, Japanese, and Chinese New Year. Some cleaning rituals consist of thorough soap-and-water sessions; some involve spirits and smoke; some combine physical and metaphysical elements.

Spring-cleaning is a traditional form of cleansing. In ancient Persia (today's Iran), celebration of the New Year involved Khaneh Tekani, which literally translates to "shaking out the house." This ritual cleansing of the home celebrates the spring season and prepares the space for a yearly visit from ancestors and recently deceased family and friends. During this cleansing, everything is washed and freshened. Rugs are cleaned, silverware is polished, new clothes are purchased, and homes are filled with hyacinth blooms.

In Scotland the New Year's celebration, Hogmanay, includes a cleaning ritual that takes place on New Year's Eve. Hogmanay's cleansing ceremony comes from the belief that until the old year has gone away, there can be no new year. To get rid of the old and make room for the new, houses are thoroughly scrubbed, and burning juniper bushes are carried through the house, where the smoke is believed to remove any lingering sicknesses.

Smoke is also used in the Native American tradition of smudging, a method of clearing out negative energies (walking, fasting, praying, and talking with a shaman are other methods). A smudging ceremony involves burning dried plants such as sage, tobacco, and sweetgrass. As the sweet smoke rises in the air and moves into all corners of a building, it cleanses the space of negativity, creating room for serenity and repose and putting to rest worries and concerns.

As you move through your CLEANSE phase, you'll be sweeping and polishing the surfaces and exteriors of things. Why not integrate a metaphysical ceremony to rid the house of any spiritual "dust"? Whether you use one of the cleansing ceremonies I have outlined above or create your own unique ceremony, choose a method that makes you feel connected, supported, and uplifted.

EXERCISE: SMUDGE YOUR SPACE

Bundles of sage and sweetgrass can be easily purchased online or at specialty shops. Native Americans believe that this ceremony clears the space and reminds us of the sacred, elevating our senses and our intentions to a place of purity. When you light your bundle of sage, carry a bowl to catch the ashes. You can voice your intentions or just meditate on them; when I do a smudging at my home, I speak about clearing the space and restoring it to the beauty and the vibration of love. I ask that all negative energies leave the space and the space be returned to a more neutral place and loving space. I usually walk around my home in a clockwise direction to symbolize the flow of forward motion and evolution.

The important thing here is not what you say — it's how you feel. Your intentions will help you focus and infuse your space with love and kindness. Fill the space with your intention, and you will see how it changes.

Home and History: Sowden House and the Black Dahlia

Sowden House, the Los Angeles home that I have lived in for nearly a decade, has been a source of great growth and joy for me. It carries with it the sepia-toned memories of fond times gone by — and a disturbing history. When I bought and revamped Sowden House, I was very aware of its architectural history; the truth about its former occupants had yet to surface.

Over the months after I moved into this gorgeous home, despite all the changes I had made, something still felt off, and I could not figure out what it was. The house was magnificent, and the restoration I had done — the result of the full SoulSpace process — had incorporated many elements that would support my dreams, such as a koi pond for meditation, a fire pit that would bring the fire element into my area, something that was very important to me, and a serene room with a beautiful desk where I could write.

My dreams were coming true — I was meditating daily while

the vibrant orange and red fish circled and dipped in the pool in front of me, I was sitting by the fire in the evenings and letting its power give me power, I was using the writing room to really refine and consider the SoulSpace process. But when I walked around the house, away from the kitchen, down the corridor that passed the room that held my gorgeous new aquarium, full of sea apples and living corals and fish I was still learning the names of, I would be overcome by uncomfortable feelings. The aquarium room was beautiful — and it made me feel terrible. The entire corridor was full of a dark energy I wanted desperately to avoid. For a long time, I did just that: I avoided that section of my home. I almost didn't realize I was doing it, until my friend Dena came over. We spent a few hours hanging out and talking, and then she said something that stopped me cold. "Why don't you ever spend time in the aquarium room?" she asked.

While the aquarium had been a recent addition that I was very excited about, we never spent any time looking at it, even though it was a lovely sitting room — we were always in the kitchen, or outside, or in the bedroom.

I was taken aback, and so I decided to do a full assessment, with Dena walking me through as a coach and supporter. I started at the farthest room, the bedroom, and spent time touching the walls, the objects, the furniture, trying to figure out the source of my discomfort. I went through each room in this way, and all I felt was positive, good, and hopeful. But when I got to the aquarium room, in particular the far corner, I was overcome by a sense of despair that made me back away.

"What does it feel like?" asked my friend. In touch with a greater perception than many of us have, she pressed me even though she could see that I didn't want to talk about it.

"It feels heavy," I said. "It feels wrong. It feels like I am stuck in quicksand, like something very bad is happening and I can't stop it."

This realization was both terrifying and upsetting for me. I am so connected to the idea of being "at home at home" that the dawning knowledge that there was something "other" in my home that was making me feel like a stranger there, even if it was only in one hallway, was not working for me. For a while after this experience, I was consumed by the hallway. Instead of ignoring it, I would walk by at every opportunity, practically daring the spirit to come out. I never saw anything manifest itself, but I did feel an eerie sensation every time I passed through that area.

Then *Black Dahlia Avenger* was published; it was given to me by a friend who had read it and recognized that the house described was my house, Sowden House. Written by a man named Steve Hodel, whose family had lived in Sowden in the 1940s, the book is a lengthy report of the crimes of Hodel's father, Dr. George Hodel. The book alleges that the doctor perpetrated a famed Los Angeles crime — the Black Dahlia murder — that had gone unsolved for more than half a century.

In 1947, a year after the Hodel family moved into the house in Los Angeles that I now own, a twenty-two-year-old woman named Elizabeth Short was found dead in LA. Not only had she been murdered; she had been surgically cut up — likely at the skilled hands of a doctor. The case was gruesome and very public, but while there were many suspects, such as Orson Welles and the infamous "Bugsy" Siegel, nobody was ever officially charged with the murders.

Steve Hodel opened my eyes to the kind of person that had been living in my home. He claims that his father killed not only

Elizabeth Short but also other women, and that Short was killed in Sowden House. The book talks about the possible murders committed by Dr. Hodel and details the abuse he heaped on his own family in the house, sexual and otherwise, such as allowing his young daughter to be sexually abused by a number of prominent figures during parties at the estate.

I was shocked and I was horrified, but I also had a new understanding about why that corridor and room felt so disturbing to me — that was where the abuse had happened. It was clear that my space needed a thorough CLEANSE so that I could reconnect with it. And it wasn't about bleach and elbow grease — it was about something much more intangible, whether you call it bad energy, spirits, or mojo.

I hired a Native American shaman to heal the space and clear the energy. He performed ceremonies and clearings to release the energy that seemed to be stuck in the space. He took out his sage and incense and lit them on fire, chanting as he walked, singing his songs to gently assist the spirit that was lingering in the house. On a certain level it felt strange, and yet it also felt very comforting.... Energy exists on many levels, and I was willing to do anything I could to clear this space.

I was determined to make sure that Sowden House would be free of its past so that I could live my life there without being haunted by someone else's unfinished business, so I also hired a priest to perform an exorcism. He came in with holy water and a Bible, and wandered throughout, sprinkling the water and reciting prayers as if he was speaking directly to the dark spirit.

Whatever they did, it worked. The next time I walked into the room with the aquarium, I was able to sit back in the comfortably designed seats and watch the fish swim slowly behind the glass, peaceful and serene.

Cleaning isn't only about getting rid of grit and mildew; it is about reinvigorating your psychic connection to your space and the energy you feel emanating from it and within it. By clearing the air, so to speak, of any malevolent, ancient, or just out-of-place auras or spirits, you make room for fresh, new, healthy feelings and connections to stream in and take their place. Why allow a spiritual invader to make you feel uncomfortable in the home you live in?

The idea of ritualistic cleansing is certainly not a new one for humankind; it has existed for many thousands of years, in most places where people have settled to create communities.

EXERCISE: MAKE CLEANING A PREMEDITATED ACTION

Before you grab the mop, take a moment to consider how a thorough spring-cleaning affects the way you feel about your home.

- What does it do for your spirit to really get in the corners and eradicate all the dust and crumbs?
- What old feelings might still be lingering in your home? What do you want to put to rest? What do you want to create space for?
- How might cleansing your home, using elbow grease and/or a ritual you find or imagine, make it feel that it is truly yours?

Cleansing to Renew and Restore Your Home

As you cleanse, pay attention to details, much as you did during ASSESS. No matter how thorough you were on your initial walk-throughs, getting down on your hands and knees is the best way to notice things you missed, the tiny details that will come together to create your SoulSpace. During CLEANSE, you don't need to repaint every room — you do need to oil a squeaky door, clear away the crumbs, and finally replace those burnt-out light-bulbs. Use the following checklist to focus your efforts.

HOUSEHOLD TASKS TO ADDRESS — RIGHT NOW, TODAY!

- ❑ Frame pictures: If you have acquired new prints and love them enough to keep them, show them off at their best by framing them.
- ❑ Dust in all the corners: Yes, it makes a difference.
- ❑ Repot houseplants that have outgrown their current homes: Take care of your indoor garden.
- ❑ Wash the windows: See your brighter future and let the sun in.
- ❑ Touch up any furniture nicks: Check your local hardware store for the appropriate products.
- ❑ Throw out old mail: Put it in two piles, "Deal With" and "Trash/Recycle." Then get to it.
- ❑ Repair a leaky faucet: Wasting water is the opposite of loving the earth.
- ❑ Repair a squeaky stair: Keep stairwells safe and secure.
- ❑ Make sure gutters are clean: Drainage counts as flow!
- ❑ Sweep the porch: Your outdoor space is part of your SoulSpace.
- ❑ Repair those clothing items that need it: hems, buttons, dry cleaning — if it's in your closet, make it ready-to-wear.

❏ Get rid of mugs with cracks or chips: Why start your morning looking at something less than lovely?

❏ Polish the silver: And don't wait until the holidays to use it — every day you're alive is a special occasion that deserves a high shine.

LET THE SUNSHINE IN

Once a month, no matter what the season, I make sure to open all the windows and doors in my home to let the sunshine in and any mustiness out. Bringing in fresh air renews your space, making it ready for the future to fill it.

CLEAN GREEN

During CLEANSE, you'll want to spring-clean your home thoroughly — even if it's the dead of winter! Sweep, scrub, polish, and wash. Ideally, as you cleanse your environment, you are making your home a safe and healthy place, full of scents such as lavender and lemongrass instead of the fake chemical odors that we used to associate with "clean."

The cleaning aisles at grocery stores are loaded with products containing harsh chemicals and artificial scents, but nowadays you have the option of instead choosing from a host of cleansers that are effective as well as gentle on you, your family, your home, and the environment. Natural and organic cleaning products are increasingly easy to find at supermarkets and hardware stores — or you can take matters into your own hands and make your own cleansers from natural products that you probably already have on your shelves. From basics like baking soda and vinegar to summer classics like lemon juice, turn what you use to make lunch and dinner into what you use to make the windows and tables shine. Talk about double duty!

BAKING SODA: This common household product in the familiar bright yellow box doesn't just deodorize your refrigerator — it doubles as a nonabrasive scouring cleaner for surfaces

WHITE VINEGAR: Not just for salad dressing, white vinegar also works on grease, mildew, and wax buildup

LEMON JUICE: Eradicates dirt, tarnish, and most household bacteria

KOSHER SALT: For use on surfaces that require extra scouring

HYDROGEN PEROXIDE: Generally antibacterial and antiviral and can be used as a general cleaner

BORAX POWDER (SODIUM BORATE): A natural mineral that cleans, deodorizes, and disinfects

WASHING SODA (SODIUM CARBONATE): This great caustic cleaner cuts grease and removes stains from clothes; it is also good for bathroom tiles — but don't forget to wear gloves while using it!

CORNSTARCH: Works as a window cleaner, a furniture polish, and a carpet shampoo

DIY Cleansers

Doing it yourself is all the rage, and not just when it comes to knitting sweaters or baking bread from scratch. Cleaners, polishes, and shiners can all be formulated from common household products, so mix it up yourself with the following recipes. Some of the ingredients, such as vinegar and baking soda, you'll probably have around. Borax and washing soda can be found in most hardware stores or supermarkets or can be ordered online. Wooden furniture, counters, sinks, laundry — getting them clean has never been easier, healthier, or more fun to brag about to your friends.

ALL-PURPOSE CLEANER
½ cup vinegar
½ gallon water

Mix and store in a bottle for cleaning showers, fixtures and surfaces, windows and mirrors.

DISHWASHER SOAP
1 part Borax
1 part washing soda

Mix and store. For hard water, use more washing soda.

LAUNDRY DETERGENT
1 cup Ivory Snow soap
½ cup washing soda
½ cup Borax

Mix and store. Use 1 tablespoon for light loads and 2 tablespoons for heavy loads.

FURNITURE POLISH FOR VARNISHED WOOD
½ cup warm water
a few drops of lemon essential oil

Mix well and spray onto a cotton cloth to dampen it; wipe furniture with the damp cloth and polish/dry with a dry cloth.

FURNITURE POLISH FOR UNVARNISHED WOOD
2 teaspoons olive oil
2 teaspoons lemon juice

Mix well and apply a small amount to a soft cotton cloth. Make sure the oil has penetrated the cloth fully, then polish furniture with the cloth.

| EXERCISE: CONNECT WITH YOUR REFRESHED SPACE |

In the previous two stages, we wrote letters to our things, using them as a focus for our strongest emotions. In CLEANSE, we continue on this theme, but this time we work to connect with our space at large, now that we have taken the time to renew it. How did cleansing your home make you feel? Did it shift your associations with any rooms in your home or any of your belongings? Did it make you want to "spring-clean" your space on a more regular basis? Did you discover any more things that needed to be released? How did metaphysical cleansing shift the energies in your home?

By cherishing our space, we cherish ourselves. By caring for our homes, we care for ourselves. It is important to create space for new opportunities and experiences, and in part 2 we will begin to take steps to fill that space. In this chapter, before we move forward, we acknowledge that by cleansing and respecting what we already have, we show ourselves all that we have to be grateful for, right here, right now.

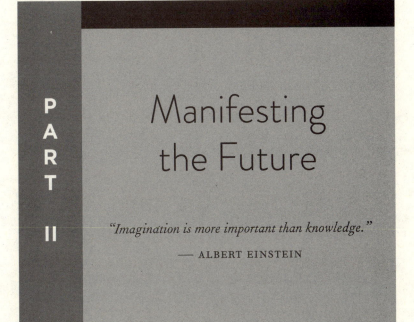

PART II

Manifesting the Future

"Imagination is more important than knowledge."

— ALBERT EINSTEIN

STAGE 4: DREAM
STAGE 5: DISCOVER
STAGE 6: CREATE

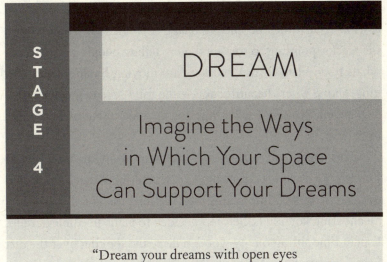

DREAM

Imagine the Ways in Which Your Space Can Support Your Dreams

"Dream your dreams with open eyes
and make them come true."

— T. E. LAWRENCE

Everything starts with a dream. Every tree starts with a seed. What if your dreams are the seeds that will grow the rest of your life? What if you must water your dreams by holding on to them and never letting them go? What if the only difference between the people who realize their dreams and the ones who don't is that the former never give up?

I am watching a yellow truck move dirt from one part of the yard to another, its mechanical fist opening and closing, collecting the heaps of ground and depositing them in a dark pile that is growing slowly and steadily.

The process takes time; it is noisy; it requires the input and assistance of other people. A shaggy-haired man runs around the trucks, pointing to trees and men, telling people where to put what. In another corner, workers are moving boulders and digging a pond where beautiful koi — the fish I love to meditate near at Sowden House — will frolic for the enjoyment of my guests in Hawaii.

This is part of creating the fulfillment of my dreams. And as I watch my dreams take shape, I remember how much fun it was to imagine this all into being. Before I had the idea for delicate, meandering koi ponds, before I decided to plant an edible garden, I spent time sitting on my wooden deck and looking over the dirt field in front of me. Now it feels as if the ponds and gardens were always meant to be here; before, I just wasn't sure. The vision existed deep inside me but hadn't surfaced yet, and so I could not manifest it into a clear plan.

I began to collect images for a dream board, a useful tool you'll learn about in this stage, and I sat on my porch, staring at the land, almost begging it to reveal its true nature to me. Would I put in a bunch of palm trees for shade, and string hammocks between them? Or did the area need to be used as a parking lot? Would a tennis court work? Another swimming pool? Would it be a serene space where my guests would get massages or an active environment where they would learn about the history of the island they were visiting? Or would it be full of hardwood trees and picnic benches? The road to inspiration can be challenging, difficult, and frustrating at times. I like to think that the universe throws up those roadblocks to challenge us to see how committed we are to our dreams and make us ready to fulfill our true destinies.

Use Your Dreams to Map Your Reality

I spent a lot of time thinking about what I would do with this area. I realized that while I wanted it to be beautiful, I didn't want it to be untouchable; I didn't want it to be a manicured space where we couldn't do anything. I wanted it to enrich our experience, complete our experience, be a viable part of our experience here in Hawaii.

I sat down and set aside a box that I would use to house my references for my dream board, and over the next few days I filled it with images that I clipped from design magazines I had around the house and photos I had taken while traveling. I then glued the images to a piece of cardboard from a box we had used to move dishes and pans from LA to Maui. In the upper right-hand corner, I placed island-themed images: the ocean, palm trees, thatched-roof huts. In the middle, a giant fish. In the upper left-hand corner, a farmhouse and a field of lettuce, right next to an orchard. On the bottom, more ocean, and a big silver faucet. I didn't know why the image of the faucet had spoken to me, but the purpose of a dream board is not to know but to feel. It's about evoking a feeling, an essence and an expression of emotion, because pictures sometimes express more fully what words strain to convey.

One thing I knew was that I was obsessing over water. I always pay attention to the quiet voice inside me. I feel as if it is my soul whispering to me — giving me clues — to move me toward realizing all that I have ever dreamed of. In this case, it was simple: I missed the water. This might sound silly, given that I was on an island surrounded by miles of ocean, with jaw-dropping views of the Pacific Ocean. But if you consider that the property is situated three miles up a volcano, far from water sources, my yearning to be closer to a water source might make more sense. I had already designated a space for a massive swimming pool surrounded by black lava rock, and apparently I wasn't done. I needed to have water elements incorporated around the property that would be very visible from all the different areas, not just in the main square.

— The other goal had to do with the land. We were sitting on so much land, and one of the things that gave us the most pleasure — aside from the view — was the abundance of fruit-bearing trees. Picking avocados and putting them into a salad; using the silver tool our neighbor gave us to open a young coconut from the tree right in front of our bungalow and drink the water; collecting macadamia nuts from under the laden branches of the tree and smashing them open with a hammer — these activities were satisfying and nourishing, and helped us feel as if we were truly a part of where we were. We wanted our guests to have the same experience, to get reengaged with the land, with the bounty of Mother Earth.

Jason and I started talking about the possibility of creating a huge edible garden, and then I had the good fortune to encounter a passionate young man who had helped create a gorgeous and inspiring organic farm in Hana, a rich, green tropical wonderland in the south of Maui. During my DREAM phase we went on a hike in Hana to open our minds to the possibilities of what we could accomplish. We walked through a bamboo forest and ate ripe, perfumed fruit from the trees and the vines — tangy red and yellow passion fruit, sweet abiu, and fragrant Surinam cherries, dark and red with delicate ridging. The flavors stayed in my memory as we cooled off under a waterfall...

Before we finalized the plans for our property, I went back and looked at the dream board I had put together. The board was very focused and repetitious: farmhouses, trees, plants, fruit, and food mixed in with pictures of the sea, of the coastline, of people on boats. I stared at the faucet I had featured so prominently, and realized that when you turn on a faucet, you get...water.

When we are in our DREAM phase, we are open to the suggestions and hints that the world offers, and the world understands our openness and sends us everything we need to make our dreams come true. What I saw on my dream board, plus the inspiration we found in that fruit-filled garden in Hana, showed me what I needed to do with the dirt field. Tennis could wait. The parking lot could go somewhere else. What we needed was water, to bring us closer to the waters that surround this bountiful volcano on which we live, and we needed fruit trees, fruit vines, and vegetable gardens, all the bounty of the land, to bring us closer to the land, the rich soil, and our home, and to connect us to a sense of greater abundance.

EXERCISE: LET THE WORLD INSPIRE YOU

This one is simple. Instead of sitting in your living room worrying about how to have big dreams, take a breather. Go outside and see other people's dreams in action. Be a part of the larger world and see what resonates for you, what takes on a special glow when your eye falls upon it. What will inspire you?

- Visit local museums and galleries: From contemporary pieces to statues from ancient Egypt, the relics of the present and the past often hold clues.
- Take a drive to nowhere at all: What will you see on the way?
- Take a walk in the park or a hike in the woods: How

does it feel to be surrounded by nature? What can you do at home to inspire the same feelings?

- Go to real estate open houses: Others might not have the same dreams as you; it is always interesting to see how other people fill a space!
- Try new restaurants and clubs: Surround yourself with sounds, textures, and tastes.
- Visit a new town or a new neighborhood: What new architectural details, shops, or restaurants can you find?

Every Dream Can Be Made Real

Not every dream of water ends in a new pond being dug; not every dream about connecting to the land involves uprooting and replanting trees. While I was working with my client Rachael, I was amazed to see how similar the imagery on our dream boards was. Mine, in Maui, was filled with water and fresh fruit and vegetables; hers, in New York City, was also full of water and beach imagery and trees and produce. Rachael is a young agent at a Manhattan literary agency who works a desk job, at a cubicle, under fluorescent lights. She travels underground, on the subway. Her home is in a building on a busy street with no backyard, no front yard, and no garden. She exercises in a gym. She gets her entertainment in restaurants and at movie theaters and bars. For someone who spends so much of her time *indoors*, I was amazed at how much of her dream life was set *outdoors*.

I asked her about this contradiction, and she explained that she was already aware of it. "I grew up in the city, and I've always dreamed of living in the country, near a lake, or somewhere quiet by the beach. But I also want this career, and right now I feel like I need to be in New York City to make it happen. One day I know I will have another life, but right now this is it."

Rachael was consciously giving up an important piece of herself in order to embrace another part of herself. What we needed to do was give her home a feeling of spaciousness, of natural connection, of the outdoors. By letting her dreams be much bigger than the space that could contain them, we were able to glean the clues we needed to incorporate those dreams into her current apartment in the later SoulSpace stages. The shifts we made included replacing her mass-produced furniture with pieces that she acquired slowly on trips to New England; these included a beautiful handmade sleigh bed and a matching dresser. Hanging planters in the kitchen made her feel more "country" even though she didn't have a porch with a rocker out back; a membership to a local CSA — community-supported agriculture — gave her a box of fresh eggs, herbs, and produce each week that made her feel as if she lived next door to a farm instead of a boutique. And a woman she met via the CSA introduced her to an organization that welcomes urbanites to their farm to help garden and maintain the land.

Now, in between vacations to Vermont and Maine, Rachael always has reminders of the natural world she loves so much. This gives her the balance she needs to maintain her city life as she moves toward having the resources to fulfill her dreams by moving to the country.

What Do You Dream About?

Rachael was consciously choosing to be a city mouse even though she knew she wanted to live somewhere much more rural: she knew what her dreams were. When I went to Maui, my intentions were mostly clear to me; at other times in my life, when my intentions were not as crystallized, my DREAM phases were tempered by a lot of confusion about who I was and what I was doing.

Sometimes our dreams and goals are not clear to us. It is easy to get tangled up in what others wish for us, or what we wished for ourselves decades or months ago. There are no dreams that are too big or too much. I believe that inside all of us are the dreams that we are meant to experience and live. Relationships, work, money, travel — all these things should be considered during the dreaming phase because there are ways to seed your home with these dreams and to infuse your space with subtle hints that will support you in getting there and receiving these dreams. After all, if you want a relationship, you need to make room inside you and your home to receive that relationship.

What are the things that you enjoy doing, right now?

The DREAM phase is the time to silence those little voices that keep you from even considering your dreams. It's time to let your imagination soar and allow your dreams to be anchored in words and pictures by creating your vision board.

EXERCISE: GET IN TOUCH WITH YOUR DREAMS

Make a list of your favorite hobbies, activities, vacation spots, or passions. These will be things you love, things you are good at, or things you want to be better at. Some examples that have come up for my clients: carpentry, yoga, cooking, gardening, working (yes, some people have truly found their passion in their work), photography, bird-watching, and football. Anything you love to do counts! You'll refer back to this list later.

Whose Dream Is It, Anyway?

Remember — just because you know how to do something well doesn't mean it is your passion. I have a client named Rebecca who is a virtuoso piano player. And you know what? She hates to play the piano.

When I started working with her, she had a giant white baby grand piano in the entranceway to her living room. It was the first thing she saw when she walked into her home and the last thing she saw when she left. Did she play that piano? No. Did she want to? No. Did others often implore her to play for them, causing her great discomfort? Yes. The piano reminded her of a childhood stuck doing what someone else wanted her to do — take piano lessons, endless, endless piano lessons — instead of having time to play, or cavort, or decide for herself what she wanted to become great at.

Her RELEASE phase involved putting that piano in a room with a door and leaving the central space in her home open and free, even though she had no idea what she wanted to have in that space instead. Her DREAM phase involved spending a lot of time reading, going to plays, going to museums — any kind of enrichment that did *not* involve music. Her dream board, interestingly, had a few images — of sculptures, clean and white and Greek — and was mostly composed of text, big, bold words that she had cut out of newspapers and magazines. "Be who you are," her dream board commanded her. "Speak up," said another clipping. Then there was a large quote from Ernest Hemingway: "There is nothing to writing. All you do is sit down at a typewriter and bleed." And under it, a picture of an old-fashioned typewriter.

Our realization? It's probably clearer to you than it was to her at that moment.

Rebecca didn't want to play or write music. She wanted to write literature.

In my experience, despite a love for the culinary arts, many of my clients have not maintained their kitchens for easy and enjoyable use. Despite a passion for yoga, they would not even have a clear corner to do a Sun Salutation. Despite a claimed fascination with gardening, one client did not have even a single plant. She said she couldn't because she had no sun. Once we got rid of a tall bookcase that blocked the only window in her tiny apartment, she was able to install a high shelf and a row of herbs and flowering plants.

Rebecca is blessed with a large home, and she did have the perfect space for writing, with an antique desk at a bay window overlooking a pond, and you know what? Despite her desire to write books, she told me she had *never* sat down at that desk to write. Until we decoded her dream board, she had not given herself permission to enter that room — which she had set up for herself when she moved into the house nearly five years before — and use it for its true purpose: writing.

If you can't be yourself at home, if you can't do what you love to do, if you don't feel creative, if you don't feel enriched and inspired — then you have a lot of work to do on your SoulSpace. In this stage, I really want you to open your mind, unfettered by ifs or what-ifs, released from can'ts and don't-know-hows. So much of what we do is tempered by boundaries — of physical space, of financial limits, of the space-time continuum. DREAM is your chance to set yourself free. Dream big. Dream true. *Dream the real you into being.*

Dream Tonight's Dream, Not Last Night's

Marc and Julie are a married couple with a fourteen-year-old son named Stefan. When Marc and Julie met, Julie was in dental school studying to become an oral surgeon, and Marc was a very successful extreme athlete. Julie was very attracted to his focus and his commitment, and Marc later said he "couldn't believe this gorgeous girl was a tooth doctor! I had never seen a dentist who looked like that!"

After a series of injuries ended his athletic career, Marc lost his way. Julie graduated from school and started practicing dentistry. Stefan was born, and Marc babysat and took care of the home while Julie spent her days doing oral surgery. By the time Marc was in his late thirties he had bounced around in a bunch of menial jobs, and Julie was basically supporting the family. Marc just couldn't settle on anything besides athletics, and, depressed about his options, he took a minor marijuana habit into the majors, putting a great strain on their relationship.

"I lecture our son about not doing drugs," Julie confided, "and his father is in the basement getting high. This just isn't working for me."

The upstairs was mostly Julie and Stefan's territory, with her magazines and his books all over the kitchen table and his bike in the foyer. The basement was Marc's lair, and it was like a treasure trove of Marc's past, with many of his sports trophies on prominent display. With no more recent successes being showcased, and no chance of recapturing the glory of his heyday, this display was more depressing than uplifting.

During their DREAM phase, I had Marc and Julie work on dream boards. With all Marc's focus on his past, I expected him to put sports-related images on the board; instead, there was a host of pictures of wooden furniture, ranging from cabinets to bed frames to tables.

Julie's images all showed neat and orderly homes that featured men and women who were attractive, professional, and put together. The center of her board was a huge dining room table, which represented her desire to have them eat dinner together "like a real family" — and the fact that she really wanted a new table.

A wooden table was the only thing their two boards had in common, and I knew it somehow had to be the key.

I looked at their dream boards, and I looked around the basement, where all Marc's trophies were displayed. He was trying to show us something, something important — what was it? I looked at the wall that held those shiny silver and gold cups, those bronze athletes straining toward perfection, lifting a tiny bat that would never connect with a tiny bronze ball — and then I saw beyond them. Or rather, under them. What I needed to notice more than those were the gorgeous polished shelves they were resting on.

"Those are beautiful," I said to Marc. His entire face lit up — it was incredible.

"Marc made those," said Julie.

"Seriously?" I said.

Marc led me into a corner of the garage where, next to their car, he had a tiny workshop squeezed in. He had built those gorgeous shelves with virtually no space to maneuver and with old, practically rusty tools.

"Marc is always puttering around in here," said Julie. "He fixes things around the house all the time."

I was amazed. During the first three phases, nobody had ever mentioned this to me. Sure, we had visited the garage during the assessment. But with their large station wagon parked inside, the workshop had been invisible. And despite all the questions I had asked, Marc's carpentry skills had been just as hidden as that workshop.

Here, I thought to myself, here is the key.

Marc's SoulSpacing clearly would involve turning his garage into a workspace where we could allow his creativity to flourish so that he could continue fixing things around the house and build cabinetry, furniture, and so on. His breakthrough came to the surface because of his dream board. Through his filling a book with photos of images that inspired him and that he connected with, we were able to put the pieces together and realize that the best thing for him was not to re-create his past goals via a fitness room or a basketball hoop in the backyard. The best thing would be to turn the garage into a workspace where he could make his new goals come to fruition.

Your Dream Board

Who are you in your wildest dreams? What do you do, what do you cherish, what are you excited by, who do you spend your time with? Do you live alone on an island? In the middle of a big city in a tall building? Do you make time to see your family more? Are you more focused on your career? Do you quit your banking job and become a hula dancer? Do you abandon your position as a pet psychologist and become a firefighter? Do you leave Colorado for California, California for New York, New York for the Sahara?

The dreams I am talking about here are the dreams that represent your soul's expression, your soul's journey — not the dreams that have been marketed to you about what you should want and can't have. Your true dreams are the ones you stay connected to, and the journey is as fulfilling as the attainment of the dream.

Sometimes realizing your dreams involves turning your life upside down; sometimes it involves digging for clues to help you make your big-city studio feel like a sun-drenched faraway locale, or your Denver ranch house like a Palm Springs paradise, full of white and light, or your San Francisco townhouse more like a Manhattan loft.

Your dreams are personal to you. Like your fingerprints, they are yours and yours alone. The same goes for your dream board: it should reflect your wishes, your hopes, your needs — not someone else's dreams or wishes for you.

As you start creating your dream board, it's important to let your mind go and to reach for impulses and feelings instead of things that "make sense." Go for what attracts you, whether images or words or phrases that you feel drawn to, that give you a yes inside. Dive below the surface of your mind and your most readily voiced opinion, and reach for the purity of what you impulsively say yes to. If you create your vision board in an almost meditative way, you will find your hand just reaching out, and your mind moving with the flow. Trust yourself. Don't create a story — let the pictures do the work for you. Trust me — you have a story that wants to be told.

Dream Board Supplies

You will need a lot of magazines — design magazines or any other type. You may also want to bring personal photos to the table, or pieces of fabric with colors and textures that you love, that truly appeal to you. The additional supplies will depend on the shape and form you would like your dream board to take — in some cases, it won't be a board at all; it may be a binder, a box, a book, a display, or even a digital file instead of something physical. Whatever feels right for you is the right choice.

BOARD: For a board, you can use foam core board, poster board, or corkboard, along with glue or rubber cement, tape, and markers or paints. You can frame your board or not. Again, what works is about what works for you.

BINDER: For a binder, you'll want a hole puncher and some folder pockets as well as paper, glue, tape, and so on

BOX: For a box, you'll want a sturdy box with a lid.

BOOK: You can make your dream board portable by using a composition notebook that you can tuck into your bag or keep in your car.

DISPLAY: You can buy a clothesline and pin your images across the room or come up with some other creative way to make your dream board into an installation.

DIGITAL: Borrow some techniques from technology to create a digital dream board to keep track of your online inspirations. Use a scanner to import images from magazines or photographs, and keep them filed together using a program like iPhoto, an online system like Picasa, or imaging software like Photoshop.

EXERCISE: CREATE YOUR OWN DREAM BOARD

Assemble your materials in a quiet space. Take a few moments to think about what you want to accomplish. The vision board that you are putting together is meant to connect you with your soul's expression of you in your space, in your home. Flip through the magazines that you have gathered and cut out the images, words, and phrases that inspire you. Add them to the stack of personal photos and fabric swatches that you selected. Once you have a large stack, go through the items one more time and assess each one to see if it truly appeals to you on a deep level. Eliminate those that don't. If you make sure the pictures are charged with your emotions and feelings of passion, you will begin to manifest the things they represent. Then start arranging the clippings where you feel they belong on your vision board. Don't think about where they should go; allow your intuition to guide you in placing them, and trust that your board will reveal something important to you when you are finished. If you're working with a board, binder, or book, the next step is to glue the images down.

Once you have finished your dream board, step back and see what it is trying to communicate to you. Do certain colors dominate? Is a particular style prevalent? Does it reflect dreams or desires that you haven't explored?

Keep your vision board in a place where you will see it often so that it can inspire you and remind you of what your soul wants you to express.

──Dream Board for Couples

If you are working with your partner or spouse to create a shared home, you may want to make a joint dream board. Explaining the significance of the images to your partner can be a wonderful way for him or her to explore some of your inner dreams, and vice versa.

EXERCISE: DREAM YOURSELF DOING

Once you have discovered your muses, work to make them real. What do you want to do in your new space? Look at your dream board and the list you made earlier for the exercise "Get in Touch with Your Dreams" (see page 102). The next step is to reflect on how you can incorporate these images, colors, textures, ideas, and dreams into the design of your SoulSpace. Using the following ideas as guides, brainstorm and write down ways that you can adapt your home to cater to your wildest dreams.

- Dream of being a master woodworker? Focus on creating a space where you can work with wood and safely store tools.
- Dream of being a yogi? Create a quiet corner where you can roll out your mat.
- Dream of being on *Iron Chef*? Take steps to create a well-organized, well-appointed kitchen.
- Dream of growing the world's biggest squash? Focus on building raised garden beds or establishing an area for container gardening.
- Dream of working for yourself? Create a comfortable space where you can be productive and feel professional.
- Dream of being the next Ansel Adams? Display your work. Purchase software or build a darkroom.

Dream your new life into being! Pursue your passions by creating a home that supports your passions.

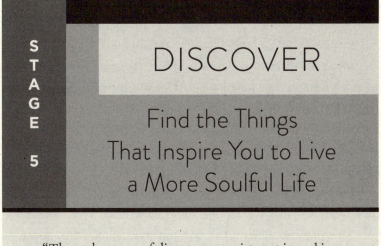

DISCOVER

Find the Things That Inspire You to Live a More Soulful Life

"The real voyage of discovery consists not in seeking new landscapes but in having new eyes."

— MARCEL PROUST

Your voyage of discovery doesn't start now — it started when you were a child, as soon as you took in your first sensations of the world, as soon as you realized that there were things you liked more than other things, tastes you wanted to enjoy again, toys you wanted to hold or chew or throw across the room. As soon as you knew you liked one thing over another — vanilla over chocolate, strawberries more than blueberries, LEGOs more than wooden blocks — you began exercising your power to discover what is right for *you*.

Discovery is about finding the pieces out there in the world

that will complement and nourish the underused parts of ourselves that we want to encourage and bring out into the light.
When people talk about "finding themselves," they are often
talking about discovering new affinities that feel perfectly natural even though they may have just been exposed to that particular subject, style of dance, or manner of architecture. When you
venture out into the world and expose yourself to places where
you don't normally go, things start talking to you. I have had that
experience time and time again: when I simply open myself to the
possibilities, things make themselves known to me — as if it was
they who were discovering me and not the other way around.

This phase builds on the previous one, encouraging you to
trust your dreams and your impulses. If you find yourself drawn
to the other side of town, follow your desires — maybe there is a
new piece of you waiting in another zip code.

DISCOVER is about taking our fantasies and incorporating
them into our daily lives via actual, tangible things we can touch
and hold, pack into the backseats of our cars, and install in our
bedrooms, kitchens, living rooms, or gardens to remind us of an
integral part of our souls. It is about recognizing the unexpected
as a kindred soul mate; about experiencing a kind of déjà vu when
you pick up an object — maybe a wooden bowl or a heavy gold
ring — that makes you know you need to bring that thing home
and hold it or wear it every day.

I once wandered into a rock crystal warehouse that was next
door to the restaurant where I had just eaten lunch. I had no idea
that I needed some crystals in my life until I reached out and
touched truly amazing pieces of amethyst and quartz. I had been
aware that I wanted to feel more connected to the earth when I
was in my home, and when I touched the crystals, I was imbued
with a feeling of connectedness, a feeling of being one with the

earth. I brought them home, and every day they remind me to take the time to connect with the planet.

The Two Sides of Discovery

A true SoulSpace incorporates both intention and serendipity, the beauty of conscious design and the magic of accidents. Sometimes we think we know what we want — as in, "I need a table" — and we can look for it. Other times, our imaginations are stimulated and we have to catch the fever, as it were — as in, "Those flowers are pretty! I should buy them!" To help you establish your home in a way that reflects each of these elements, I've separated the DISCOVER phase into two components: I call the two sides "intentional discovery" and "imaginative discovery."

INTENTIONAL DISCOVERY

When we connect our realities to the soaring heights of our imaginations, our day-to-day lives can be uplifted from the mundane to the extraordinary, and our dreams can be anchored to something real so they don't just fly up and away, into the heavens. In this stage, you're going to think about the dreams you uncovered in the preceding stage and figure out how to make them real.

If in your DREAM phase you considered your cramped studio apartment and thought, "I wish I lived in a glass dome," now is the time to translate that into "I want to live in a space that is awash with light." By realizing that what you need is more light instead of a crystal palace, you can use the DISCOVER phase to find lamps, chandeliers, lighter curtains, mirrors — anything that can increase or magnify the amount of light streaming into your home. In DISCOVER, you might find a beautiful chandelier that makes you feel wonderful (in CREATE, the next stage, you will worry about the installation and take care of the practical to-dos).

If you thought about how much you hate working in a corner of the den and concluded, "I want to turn the entire first floor of my home into my office," now is the time to figure out how to ask your husband if he minds giving up the living room, the kitchen, and the den, or translate your wish into "I want to work in a space that is professional, handsome, and well appointed." By realizing that what you need is a more spacious and well-defined workspace, you can focus your efforts on discovering a desk with built-in shelving and a roll-top for when you aren't working. Or maybe you'll realize that the den, which is often used, and the living room, which you rarely use, since you tend to meet friends at restaurants, can be combined so that the living room can be turned into your office, and your work can take place in some actual space.

If you dreamed about savory, tasty morsels or luscious pies and tarts, and thought, "I wish I could quit my job and go to culinary school," either download some applications or translate that into, "A beautiful kitchen would let me explore my passions for cooking right here at home."

By realizing that you can bring your dreams home, now, without taking out a student loan or changing your whole career — although I encourage you to do both if that is where your heart is reaching! — you can integrate your fantasies into your life and make them real. All you need is to gather some beautiful cookware, a shelf full of cookbooks, and some artisanal ingredients and spend a lazy Sunday afternoon...

Intentional discovery is about finding objects that you love that remind you of your dreams. It is about seeding your space with things whose beauty resonates with you. In my dining room,

I have a large oil painting titled *The Unification of Humanity*. I love its rich textures, the skilled hand of the artist, and the way it looks on the wall — but I also love how it makes me feel and what it makes me think about. We are all here to do our part in bringing the human family back together, and this idea has been a deep guiding force along my personal path. I chose the painting because it reflects this idea and reminds me of what is truly important to me. On your DISCOVER journey, look for objects and pieces that hold an idea of what you want to become or that embody an important way of being that you would like to master.

If you love going to Caribbean beaches, what can you discover that will remind you of those wonderful adventures at the shore? If you love snorkeling and only get to go once a year, perhaps there is a beautiful aquarium out there just waiting for you to find it — or for you to allow it to find you.

IMAGINATIVE DISCOVERY

In this phase you are like Christopher Columbus, setting sail across a broad sea to an only-dreamed-about new land. He went somewhere unexpected, and a whole new stage of human history unfolded. What new worlds are waiting out there for you? Use this phase to make the dream of you real by embodying it in objects in your SoulSpace.

You have learned a lot about yourself through this process, and you most likely have a sense of what you need to discover. Armed with this information, you can let your imagination lead the way as you explore the unknown. Oftentimes, people limit themselves to a certain style or a certain type of store because it's what they're used to. They get stuck in styles because they have not been exposed to other styles. Here I want you to open yourself to the unfamiliar and shop in places you wouldn't normally go to. Do you tend toward clean, modern lines? Investigate antique shops to see if you might fall in love with an inlaid trunk that someone brought over from the old country on a steamer line that no longer exists. Do you tend toward heavy wooden antiques? What about visiting specialty stores in your neighborhood to see if a red lacquer chest might lend some pizzazz to your old-fashioned entryway? Vintage shops, secondhand stores, flea markets, Craigslist, estate sales — put yourself in places where items are waiting to be adopted.

Imaginative discovery doesn't just happen out in the world. It is also about keeping your eyes open in your own home to re-imagine familiar objects and discover new and surprising ways to use them. Would a dining room chair be perfect in a corner of the bedroom? Can that old guitar that you loved be restrung and used to teach your daughter a few chords? Or can you hang it as art in the playroom? What do you have that you could be using more or better or differently?

During our renovations in Maui, we tore a building down and discovered an old water tank that had been there since 1909. We dragged it out of the wreckage of the building and laid it on its side — and I realized that it needed to become the base of a spectacular dining room table. You never know how something can be used!

INTENTIONAL DISCOVERY AT WORK

Remember Rachael? As a young agent with a burgeoning career, she couldn't leave the city; she also couldn't afford a country house to give her the balance she craved. In her DISCOVER phase, we focused on bringing the outside in.

We were constrained by space and budget; she was totally open to exploring any ideas that could lend her city environment a feeling of airiness, relaxation, and natural connection. Since Rachael was connected to farm/green, mountain, and beach elements, we had a lot to play with. She was about to leave for a vacation in Honduras, and her excitement over her upcoming trip was apparent as we navigated the aisles of the local flea market.

Intentional discovery led us to a sale on window boxes, which, when filled with plants, would enhance her view of cars and streets and buildings with a row of greenery. We chose plants recommended for their lush green foliage and low maintenance needs, as well as a jade plant that Rachael felt was calling to her. During CREATE, we made sure to get herbs so she could add some plucked-from-the-garden savor and flavor to her dinners: chives, basil, and mint did the trick for her. While in the DISCOVER phase we also found a huge mirror that could hang in the living room on the wall nearest the windows; that way, when the morning sun slanted in, the mirror would send it splashing across the room.

At a local print shop, we found two huge photographs of beach scenes. One showed sun seekers filling the sands and the water's edge as far as you could see. The other was of a wild, empty beach, with gnarly white trees backing a slim stretch of sand, with the blue waters at the base of the photo — it looked as if it had been taken from a boat. "Which one do you want?" I asked Rachael. She knew immediately.

"I see people all day," she said. "I want the empty beach. I want to come home and feel like I am there."

IMAGINATIVE DISCOVERY AT PLAY

Imaginative discovery helped us notice when a round fish tank made Rachael smile. She told me she hadn't had fish as pets since she was in grade school; perhaps it was time again. If she didn't get fish, we agreed, she could repurpose the tank as a vase or a terrarium.

It also allowed us to see her space in a new way. There was a skylight in Rachael's hallway but the landlord had boarded it up years ago. She wrote him a letter asking if he would repair it, telling herself that if he said no she would counter by offering to pay for it herself. In the end, since he was renting out another apartment on the same floor that also had a boarded-up skylight, the landlord decided he would repair both of them free of charge. This extra bit of light lent an airy feel that Rachael luxuriated in every time she moved between rooms, making the smallest, darkest part of her apartment a place where she could see the sky.

This shift helped her feel lighter in other parts of her life as well. I knew this as soon as she called me a couple of weeks later.

"How was your trip?" I asked.

"Amazing!" she said. "I was outside the whole time! And guess what? I bought a hammock. I'm going to hang it in the corner instead of getting a chair. It might look weird, but I don't care. And I did so much snorkeling! I am definitely going to get some beautiful tropical fish."

I was so proud of her! She had continued her discovery on her trip, and now every time she swung in her hammock or looked at her aquarium, she would not only feel connected to a more relaxed, outdoorsy lifestyle but also remember her wonderful experiences in Honduras, on the land and in the sea.

Finding the Tools You Need

Every person's DISCOVER adventure is as individual as his or her dream board. For Rachael, the "tools" she needed were as simple as plants, a hammock, and a print — she had a stressful career and was simply looking for a feeling of relaxation. Marc's needs were very different. When you met him, in his DREAM stage, he realized that his small garage workspace was an important part of his SoulSpace. In DISCOVER, the "tools" he needed to find were literally tools.

Your tools might be a kayak or a Bundt pan, a piano or a sewing machine, a juicer or a pair of ice skates. A couch for relaxing. A row of trees for privacy. An in-ground swimming pool. New silverware. Antique lamps. Heavy velvet curtains. A stationary bike. A mountain bike rack. The most expensive ukulele they have in the store.

In Marc's case, he already had a set of tools and a worktable, but on closer inspection, they were of very shoddy quality. Because Marc hadn't taken his "hobby" seriously, he hadn't taken his equipment or his work area seriously — even though the furniture he made was of very, very high quality.

Discovering Your Dreams Is Worth an Investment

It wasn't easy for Marc to decide to make a real investment in the workroom he had finally come around to envisioning during our DREAM sessions. At first, he approached DISCOVER with a lackluster energy, not wanting to spend the money to replace the cheap tools he was working with. He wasn't fully committed to his dream because of the cost required to begin to manifest it. I could understand it — with Julie's hard work as an oral surgeon supporting the small family, he was loath to ask her for more money "just so I can have a fancy hammer," as he explained it. But at the same time, he needed to take himself and his potential seriously enough to see his workroom as an office, as a training ground, as the facility in which he would literally build his and his family's future.

At a family meeting, Marc broke down and told Julie how terrible he felt about what had happened in the past, and how he was having a tough time resolving his past failures by asking her for *more* money. Julie told Marc that she believed in him and his dream and that she wanted him to have a workroom so he could really produce. Their son told Marc that he had saved up money from his summer job and he wanted to give it to his dad.

They didn't need to use Stefan's summer income, since Julie was making good money, but his family's excitement and support showed Marc that using their resources for this goal wouldn't be taking from them. When he made his new career a success, he would be giving to them, more than he could ever imagine. This confidence pushed Marc right through DISCOVER and CREATE, as he used the resources to put together a very professional work-space.

Seeing her husband excited about his future, seeing his face light up as he talked about how he would create his new work-room, reminded Julie of the man she had married a decade and a half ago, who knew his worth and his value. Their son, seeing his dad proud of the furniture he had built, was introduced to a father he had never met before, a far cry from the sad man who had watched television alone downstairs with a beer while Julie and Stefan ate dinner together upstairs.

A year later, when I visited their home, I noticed a beautiful dining room table in a simple Shaker style instead of their old, beat-up table. "Marc made it," said Julie, and her eyes shone with pride. I felt pretty proud myself when I looked at this family and their successful SoulSpace: Julie had her dream table, and Stefan had his dream bunk bed — crafted in their garage by Marc, who already had a contract with a local company to make five more of those tables.

DREAM and DISCOVER helped Marc reconnect to his passion so he could really embrace CREATE, which led him straight to his confidence, to his future, to his family.

Who is the excited person living inside you? We often live on automatic pilot, a setting that steals the excitement of life and discovery from us. Dream every day! Discover every day! Rip off the blinders and take a good look around! What do you want? What do you desire?

Who are you?

Letting Function Follow Form

People who love design talk a lot about "form following function." This is the idea that an object's design should be based primarily on how it will be used. Sometimes in DISCOVER we find exactly the opposite: that function follows form, that things can have uses they were not intended for because of the way they are shaped, accidentally instead of purposely. Letting function follow form is an exercise of dismissal: dismissing the labels put on things by the designer, builder, or manufacturer and letting their shape tell you how they might be integrated into your environment.

When I was choosing the furnishings for Sowden House, some decisions came to me very easily, such as the fabrics for the living room and the lamps for the master bedroom. But some were more elusive, like the table that would be used in the main dining room. Eventually, I had the entire house set up just as I wanted it — but there was still no dining room table, and so, while I could (and did) host many cocktail parties, the dinner celebration I wanted to have was on hold until I discovered the ideal table for the space.

I was also unhappy with the guest bedroom. I had done it in a lush silver, gleaming and dark and sensual, with black and white art that had a great verve and movement. But the bed was wrong. It was dark and sensual, but it didn't gleam. It didn't shine. It didn't resonate with me. It wasn't a room I was in often, and I never slept there. When I walked down the hallway it annoyed me. So those were the two things I needed to discover: the perfect table for the dining room and the perfect bed for the guest room.

NOT JUST ANY PIECE WILL DO

At different times, we have different needs. When I started putting together living spaces for the Maui project, I needed temporary furniture that was livable and inexpensive. I scoured Craigslist for deals on bamboo and rattan furniture that would be in keeping with the sensibilities of Hawaii and the bungalows we were residing in. I wasn't looking for *perfect*; I was looking for *good enough*. It's important to know which one you need! If you're living in Moscow for a semester studying Russian architecture and you need somewhere to sit, you probably need a couch that is *good enough* as opposed to *perfect*. If you are equipping your dream house and you have an unlimited budget, please, take the time to look for *perfect*. You'll know it when it speaks to you.

For Sowden House, I didn't have an unlimited budget, but I had some resources to allocate, and I wanted something perfect, a table that would really set off the space as well as be a good excuse to get people together to eat, talk, and laugh. I knew I wanted something very unusual in the space, so instead of perusing manufacturers' catalogs from Italy or checking out the latest LA design hot spots, I decided I would go downtown to the salvage yards I had heard of and shop around to see if I could get some inspiration. I really did not want to use the typical wood or metal and glass for the table; I wanted something that would serve as an art piece as well as a surface to hold our plates and cups and elbows, something that would be a conversation piece.

Going to places that are out of the way and not the "right" kind of store to go to can lead to some fun ideas. I arrived at a giant warehouse that held about 25,000 square feet of salvaged, cast-off, and found objects, and when I was about to feel overwhelmed by the scope of the merchandise, I took a deep breath. I told myself that if I went slowly and just wandered around, I might discover something incredible. I was intentionally looking for imaginative discovery. Or maybe I was imaginatively seeking intentional discovery. Either way, I knew it would be interesting to spend a few minutes checking out a store full of bizarre cast-offs. It was like a museum, full of tapestried chaise lounges and old stained glass, chess sets that looked as if they came with the ghosts of their players, and Tiffany lamps in pinks and beiges and blues. And then I saw these beautiful bronze gates. I was captivated.

I didn't need gates for any of my projects, but I just couldn't walk away. I knew I could use them for something. But what? I started asking questions about them. Where did they come from? What were they used for? The salesclerk didn't know. I started wondering how I could store them, thinking it would be easier to store them horizontally than vertically. Once my mind shifted them onto their backs, I saw them in a new way. They weren't just gates. They were a future table: topped by a sheet of glass, they would be ideal for my dining room. The patina of the old bronze and the design were perfect for the space. I sent the gates to my metal fabricator to cut and assemble the table.

Every room in your house can benefit from a touch of the unusual. A redesigned item makes a complete original and a great conversation piece. Ideally, each room should have one conversation piece — something striking or unusual that people will be sure to ask about. Intimacy often begins with a great conversation!

Use, Reuse

At another salvage emporium, among floors and floors of leftovers, rejects, and outsized building materials, I stumbled upon an amazing piece of architecture: a large metal window and dormer from an old building in New York City. The building had been built in the '20s. I just loved the window's patina, its shape, and the idea of taking a piece of architecture and redesigning it so that it could work in my home. I bought it before I knew what to do with it. While walking through my home one day, considering how to reuse this large sculptural piece, I wandered down the hallway that housed the guest bedroom with the bed I was less than fond of.

In a flash, it came to me. If I cut my newest find down and replaced the window with a mirror, I could remake it as a headboard just by adding an extension for the legs.

By leaving room to be inspired by serendipity, by taking a piece of historical architecture and reimagining it to add a richness and depth to the space in question, I did more than furnish a room. I created a feeling, a suspension of reality, a moment housed in a dream. For me, the typical or expected have no room in my SoulSpace. After all, I like living life with a sense of fantasy and over-the-top design. I like the unexpected use and the clever reuse of materials. Not only is it an environmentally sound practice, but in my experience, it is one of the keys to inspiring innovative, beautiful, and personalized design.

As you set out on your own discovery journey, it is very important to step outside your usual paths in order to create a home that marries your dreams with serendipity. Go to swap meets, furniture stores, art galleries, antique stores, fabric stores. Using DISCOVER to translate your dreams into reality is an integral part of your SoulSpace growth, and so is opening your eyes to the possibilities inherent in the unexpected. When you go seeking, bring a list of everything you think you need — and remember that sometimes what we need most will not be obvious. Be open, be loose, be relaxed, and let yourself feel your way as you go out of the way to discover your dreams and bring them home.

WEBSITES AND APPS FOR YOU TO DISCOVER

CRAIGSLIST (www.craigslist.org): Virtually everybody knows Craigslist, and everybody appreciates Craig for his great idea. Who knows what you might find — new home furnishings, or even a new home!

EBAY (www.ebay.com): eBay has more than twenty million auction or "buy it now" listings. Are your dream purchases hiding among them?

ETSY (www.etsy.com): This site offers handmade goods, as well as vintage décor, including art and furniture; it also has a "shop local" feature, which shows you sellers in your area.

ESTATESALES.NET (www.estatesales.net): Find estate sales in your area; you can also look up estate liquidation companies and sign up for their email newsletters alerting to you new sales. TIP: *Visit estate sales on the first day, and if the prices aren't just right for you, hold off and go again on the last day. You might miss some great pieces, but if you go when the sale is about to end, you might be able to negotiate 50 percent or more off.*

GARAGE SALES TRACKER (www.garagesalestracker.com): Find sales in your area. If you're looking for a specific thing, you can filter by "items for sale." The site includes embedded driving directions and also allows you to search for flea markets and/or consignment shops in your area. It offers an iPhone app too.

GARAGE SALE ROVER (garagesalerover.navigapp.com): This handy smartphone app, available for both iPhones and Androids, uses your satellite location and merges it with Craigslist ads for sales in your area.

AUCTIONZIP (www.auctionzip.com): Search for local auctions. You can filter auctions based on specific keywords, view lists of auction houses or auctioneers in your area, and request notifications of auctions.

GOODWILL (www.shopgoodwill.com): Similar in format to eBay, this site auctions off hand-picked items from Goodwill stores across the country in all categories.

ANTIQUESNAVIGATOR.COM (www.antiquesnavigator.com): This site is a great resource for finding antique stores or antique malls in your area.

EXERCISE: DISCOVER FROM THE COMFORT OF YOUR HOME

Whether you're an opera lover, a bird-watcher, or a tomato enthusiast, there are a host of magazines, websites, and blogs aimed at your demographic. These can be great resources for DISCOVER. Spend time browsing through publications that interest you while you search for discoveries for your SoulSpace. The insights you gathered in DREAM were meant to inspire your thinking to soar to new heights. The materials you will gather through this DISCOVER exercise are meant to encourage you to act, so if you find items you want on these websites or in these magazines, pick up the phone or get online and place those orders.

How to Get the Most Out of DISCOVER

Don't cut corners on DISCOVER. The first lamp you see, the first drill the clerk recommends, or the first wooden table on display is just the beginning of your discovery. Keep looking! Go out of the way, go long, go back. Take the time to find the items that sing to you. Don't settle for less. Each discovery should be something you really need, you have really fallen in love with, and you cannot wait to install in your reimagined living space. Every last item you discover should feel like an indispensable piece of your SoulSpace.

Keep in mind that DISCOVER is one of those stages that you never really leave. During your CREATE stage, which you're about to enter, you will be continually returning to DISCOVER so that you can make your dreams more real. Even after your home is "done," I hope that you will embrace and continue this journey of discovery for the rest of your life!

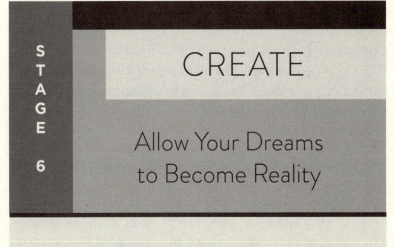

STAGE 6

CREATE

Allow Your Dreams to Become Reality

"Design is a plan for arranging elements in such a way
as best to accomplish a particular purpose."

—— CHARLES EAMES

What is beautiful to you? I'm not just talking about wall coverings or furnishings. I mean what moves you the way a gleaming kitchen excites the eye of a home chef. The way an empty room, full of usable space, sparks the soul of a dancer. The way a row of guitars makes the hand of a musician itch. When you create your home, you will focus on making concrete additions that will inspire you and encourage you to *act*.

The CREATE stage can be about many things. It may lead to rearranging a room to encourage feelings and interactions — such as turning chairs and couches so they face each other, to create natural conversation areas instead of television-viewing seating. Or you might turn your closed-in kitchen and rocky garden into an oasis for family gatherings by adding French doors, an extended patio, and an incredible barbecue station. Or CREATE might be about developing your latent talents — such as converting a den into a weaving room with a loom purchased at an estate sale.

Make Your Space Yours

How many times have we seen magazine articles with people who have turned a lighthouse into their home or made an old barn into the coolest place to live? We love and admire people who think that far out of the box and create the extraordinary out of the ordinary.

Whatever you do with your CREATE stage, make sure that you are really making your home *yours*. It doesn't matter how someone else would arrange the space — it matters what you need, what life you want to support, the goals that *you* have.

One of the best lessons I ever learned about CREATE came from a young woman I met at the wedding of a colleague of mine, a woman I had known for years and really loved and respected. When I was introduced to her little sister, a graphic designer, I was taken by how similar they appeared and how different their personalities were. My colleague was very proper, someone who always wore suits to work, heels, the works. Until I saw her in her white dress, I had literally never seen her "let her hair down." Her sister, Gita, was the complete opposite — clearly a free spirit, totally in touch with who she was and what she wanted. She was getting married the following summer, she told me, to Emil, a doctor who had just begun his residency at a hospital in Chicago. I asked where they lived, and she laughed.

"Right next door to the hospital," she said. "Practically in it. Our apartment is so small. It's really awful."

"You say that," I observed, "but you don't sound very upset." I spend so much time quizzing people about their personal spaces that it's tough to stop, even when I'm at a social engagement! Lucky for me, she was a charming young woman and seemed happy to submit to my questioning.

"We used to have a great place," Gita explained, "but we moved so he could be near the hospital. It was terrible when we moved in. Not only was I far away from all my friends, but our new apartment was so noisy. The bedroom is right over a busy street, and his shifts are at night, so he needs to sleep during the day. It was just impossible."

"Was?" I asked.

"We figured it out," she told me. "We switched the bedroom and the living room. We moved the couch into the bedroom and the bed into the living room. My sister said I was crazy, but it's been working out really well. Now the living room is small and noisy, but that doesn't bother us when we watch TV. And the bedroom is sunny and quiet. It's right off the kitchen, and there aren't any doors, so our one-bedroom feels more like a studio. But he's happier, and so am I." She waved at a tall, attractive guy in glasses who was at the bar; he waved back.

"So that was that," Gita said, moving off toward her beau. "It doesn't work for guests or for having parties, but we don't care. The apartment isn't for other people. It's for us."

For Gita and Emil, CREATE was about realizing what they disliked about their home, and being clear on what they wanted from it. They disliked the noisy bedroom; they needed a quiet room. Had Gita preferred to keep the living room for entertaining guests, they would have had an issue: there was simply not enough room to have a space meant for guests that was light and spacious, and have a quiet bedroom where Emil could get the rest he needed between his shifts. Since they were clear and united in their desires, they were able to solve the problem. Their solution would not have worked for everybody — but that's okay. It worked for them, and that's all that matters.

CREATE is not about making a room that an interior design magazine wants to photograph or your best friend wants to copy. It is about creating a space that is perfect for *you*, and consciously designed to support *your* life. As part of a young couple working toward establishing a relationship to support them for the rest of their lives, Gita was concerned not about having an office or having a party space but about nourishing her needs and Emil's needs, so that their love could have a place in which to take root and bloom. Their solution to the issue at hand was to see the space independently, instead of being limited by what it was intended for. And that is the essence of what CREATE is all about.

Don't give in to the cookie-cutter organization that so many homes have been built with! I believe that all people are extraordinary, not ordinary. Why try to fit into a mold when we can discover and create ourselves the way we truly want to be? Use your space as a laboratory for your creativity; it will give you the strength to begin taking this creativity into everything you do. Having the courage to think outside the box will help you start expressing a more radiant and beautiful you.

Your space is not just a shell for *any* person — it is *your* special place in the world. Organize its interiors with integrity. If you built your home from the ground up and worked with an architect, you were able to make decisions about every part of your space: custom-built means a custom fit. If you bought an existing structure and did renovations, you also had the opportunity to custom-fit your space to your life. If you moved into a house or apartment and did only minor updates, or, like Gita and Emil, you are renting a space and aren't going to do anything major, you might feel stuck with certain aspects of your home.

Maybe you love the kitchen but hate the way the living room ceiling slopes. Perhaps the hallways are too narrow, the basement ceiling too low, the bedrooms too small or too dark — these are the kinds of common complaints that you should and must address in CREATE. But don't worry — there are many inexpensive ways to deal with these issues. You could perhaps add a large mirror in the hallway to give the illusion that the hallway is wider than it actually is. You can add more lighting to dark rooms, and you can paint ceilings with a reflective finish to give a feeling of more height.

The important thing about CREATE is that you reconnect to the power you have inside and realize that you can use that power to make the life you want real. What better place to reconnect to your power than in your home? It is in our own homes that we can play with the magic of who we are. Let yourself create the environment you dream of so you can begin to create the life you want to live.

Coexisting via Conscious Creation

Living well with other people within a space is as important a focus of CREATE as supporting our own needs and dreams. Couples, families, roommates: all these groups of people live in shared spaces where communal dreams and individual dreams may or may not coincide. Especially during periods of economic instability, people may find themselves in shared housing even if they never expected or desired it. For my client Sharon, a widow in her late sixties, the economic downturn had an unforeseen result: it gave her a new roommate — her son.

When the value of the market slipped, so did many of Sharon's investments, and she began to have trouble making her mortgage payments. Her jewelry business, which had been thriving, lost some big accounts, and she was struggling to pay the bills. At the same time, her son Jonathan, a web developer in his late thirties, lost his job. She decided that it was silly for the two of them to struggle every month, so she invited him to come live in her house. This was not an easy decision for either of them. Sharon had grown used to her independence after ten years on her own, and Jonathan was a grown-up who was actively dating. But Sharon also liked the idea of companionship, and Jonathan did not want his mother to lose her home.

At first, although it seemed like the right decision for both of them, it also seemed that it wasn't going to work out. Feeling as if they had no choice made it hard to enjoy having each other around. Jonathan was depressed, and it showed. He moped around and could barely be bothered to get dressed every day. His insecurity only grew as the weeks went on; he stopped dating because of how he imagined the women he knew would perceive the fact that he was living with his mother.

Having Jonathan around had originally seemed like a pleasant idea to Sharon, since she had not had constant companionship for nearly a decade. As it turned out, they rarely talked. They never did anything enjoyable together. They never even ate meals together — Sharon would cook and eat early, and Jonathan would eat the leftovers at midnight. Whenever they were in the same room, Jonathan was morose and quiet and Sharon felt frustrated at her inability to draw him out.

"He does the dishes in the middle of the night," Sharon told me when we were all seated together in their spacious living room. "I wake up to a clean kitchen — that's one bonus!"

A sharp, funny woman, Sharon had hired me to reorganize her home after Jonathan's father passed away. Recently she had contacted me again to see how we could reinvigorate and reimagine the space so that it would be suitable for her and Jonathan to coexist peacefully and happily in.

As I saw it, part of the problem was the verbiage they were using, and the weight it carried. They never really talked about living together, as equals. Even though Jonathan's severance package was paying the mortgage, they both talked about the arrangement as if he was living in her house, as if she was taking care of him and he was unable to take care of himself. Really, they were caring for each other, so it was important for us to create an atmosphere that reflected that reality.

Our goal was to find potential areas of shared interest and create a space where the two could share their time. The first step was to create a space where they could eat together. The dining room was full of boxes Sharon had been storing there. When she worked through the RELEASE and CLEANSE stages, she threw much of the room's contents out and transferred the rest to a storage space in the garage. Since Jonathan was fairly handy around the house, he refinished the dining room table and reupholstered the chairs, and together they painted the walls. They made a commitment to dine together at least two days a week.

During the stages that led up to CREATE, we did the necessary homework and preparation so that we were really clear on what our goals were. Jonathan was a fine cook and, as Sharon had a bit of a green thumb, in the DREAM phase we decided it would be wonderful if she planted a small vegetable garden that he could harvest from to prepare their shared meals. DREAM also led to Sharon's realization that what she needed to revitalize her flailing jewelry business was a presence online, which was the perfect job for her web designer son. They decided to create a shared office space, where she could make jewelry and he could do his design work.

We focused our CREATE time on setting up the dining area, the garden, and the office space. In DISCOVER we had chosen upholstery material, purchased gardening supplies, and purchased the materials to make a room divider for the shared office space. They decided to put the new office in one of the spare bedrooms; his workstation went in one corner, and her craft table on the other side of the room. The room divider Jonathan built would give them each privacy if they needed it.

The first time they sat down together in their refinished dining area to eat a meal complemented by the lettuces, herbs, and other produce grown in their very own garden, Jonathan thanked Sharon profusely for inviting him to live in her home again. "It's *our* home," Sharon told him, "not mine. Ours." And as she related the story to me, she emphasized that she wasn't just being polite. The act of sharing her home with him — actively, not passively — set a tone for a new stage in their relationship. The website Jonathan created to highlight his mother's jewelry revitalized her failing business and gave him a new confidence in his own abilities. Their shared SoulSpace was a true win-win.

Making CREATE Happen

CREATE sounds as though it's the creative stage, but it's really about *muscle*. At this point, we have already identified concrete goals, dreamed big, and discovered the things we need. CREATE is about hauling boxes, using paintbrushes, reading instruction manuals — and when necessary, calling in the experts.

SELF–HOME IMPROVEMENT: A CAUTIONARY TALE

If you're under pressure from work or family responsibilities, if you are low on cash, if you cannot afford help, or if you do not have the time to devote to a big project — don't attempt a major overhaul yourself! I can't overemphasize this point. If the job is too big for your resources — whether in terms of time, know-how, physical ability, creative ability, or finances — call in an architect, contractor, or interior designer.

If you're reading this book, it's because you want to make your life better, not harder. Trust me: Anyone can buy a new couch, turn a bedroom into a sewing room, or plant a row of basil and chives. Not everyone can turn a wall into a door, a door into a window, or a window into a reading alcove. If you've never handled a drill or done tiling, do not assume under any circumstances that you have what it takes to turn a closet into a bathroom. If you've never potted a plant — well, you can do that with little to no experience.

Be a big dreamer, and a smart creator! This will save you endless tears, heartache, and dollars in the long run — I promise.

A home improvement project is a big job under any circumstances and never more so than when you've bought a foreclosed fixer-upper that needs new *everything*. Such was the case for Kate and Ben, who had been dating for three years and finally decided to buy a house following the birth of their daughter, Rose. Money was tight, and they were able to make the move with some financial assistance from their families. Sometimes the belief that you cannot afford certain things leads to unintended consequences, and this proved especially true with Ben, who decided that the best way for them to have the home of their dreams was for him to be the contractor.

Of course, something was bound to go wrong. In this case everything did. A pipe burst when they were trying to fix the plumbing, and they were without water for two days. While trying to rewire the electrical circuitry in the house, Ben nearly electrocuted himself. Then he installed an electric dryer outlet even though their new dryer ran on gas.

Thanks to their desire to improve things, the situation got a lot worse. The tension between them grew due to Ben's unrealistic need to prove he was capable of this kind of work, and his overall unwillingness to get outside help since they "couldn't afford it."

They brought me on board to help them achieve their outsized aspirations — but from day one it was clear to me that my true purpose was to help Ben scale back his ambitions. I also realized that this was a prime opportunity to have a barn raising — to get this struggling couple to capitalize on their strong community connection by asking friends and family for much-needed assistance. By putting the call out to the people who loved them, they were able to pull together the manpower to finish the renovation without anybody's having to go to the emergency room. The main goals were pulled off beautifully: their daughter's room was finished perfectly, and all the light switches worked.

I was pleased to note that the next time Ben wanted to make major changes, he called me to ask for references for legitimate contractors who could safely and efficiently complete the job. This next time, rather than imposing on their community ties, we relied on professional help to turn part of the garage into a workshop where Ben could tinker on projects and build cool things, and to turn the unfinished attic into a cozy family room filled with books and games where the whole family could unwind after a long day.

Many home improvement jobs can be accomplished with good intentions and a bucket of white paint. On the other hand, many require planning and the patience to wait until we have the resources to do the job right. In the best of situations, we don't need to ask our friends to give up a week of Sundays to help us redo the plumbing or paint the back porch; we plan projects we can accomplish with the resources at hand, whether that means hiring a crew to wallpaper the living room or choosing a strategy we can pull off ourselves.

Create Solutions to Common Complaints

There are many simple, inexpensive, and creative ways to deal with problems that you have with your space. Following are some suggestions for resolving common concerns. And remember: address the redesign of your SoulSpace at your soul's pace.

CROWDED SMALL ROOMS

- The best thing you can do is to make sure not to overwhelm the space with excess furniture or clutter. Piles of magazines or books, too many photographs, or a gallery's worth of art on the walls: all of these can combine to make a room feel even smaller than it is.
- Replace the art on one wall with a large mirror.
- Avoid heavy curtains, replacing very long or thick

window dressings with lighter, shorter, more streamlined fabrics and styles.

- In eating areas, keep tables small, or buy a dining table with a removable leaf. Tuck unused chairs into a storage space.
- Consider getting a Murphy bed to make more space in a bedroom.

Cavernous Large Rooms

- Focus on creating small, intimate areas for living and loving. Enormous spaces can be emotionally difficult to navigate — we need intimacy to feel cozy and comfortable.
- Break up the room into two sitting areas. More furniture, organized into nooks and clear areas, can encourage intimate interactions.
- Arrange furniture around focal points such as a fireplace or a view.
- Try a room divider.
- Bring in lots of books and magazines, use throw blankets, and add plants.
- Use darker colors and textured and/or patterned wallpaper.
- Hang a chandelier.
- Use music to fill the space with the desired mood.

Too Much Sun

- Make sure shades and curtains keep out the harsh midday sun. Keeping excess sunlight out of your home will help keep cooling costs low and protect your furniture and art.
- Use just the right window coverings — for example, sheers filter the sun but still allow in the light.

- Bring in plants that can use the sun — herbs and flowering plants that need a lot of sun will flourish in your bright environment.
- If your space allows, consider placing tall plants outside windows to filter the light.
- Use dimmers on light fixtures so you can control the brightness.

Not Enough Light

- Focus on adding light sources and placing mirrors in strategic places to reflect natural light. Light makes us feel awake and alive.
- Add more lamps and overhead lighting, including dimmers so you can control the brightness.
- Use candles at night to warm up the space.
- Use brighter paint colors to add lightness and an airy feeling.
- Place up-lights in the corners of dark rooms to illuminate them. These are light fixtures whose bulbs aim up instead of hanging down, creating a different atmosphere than a traditional light fixture does.
- Or embrace the shadows and create a romantic space with purposely dim lighting.

Too-High Ceilings

- Add a long chandelier.
- Hang a large mobile or other art piece in the center of the room.
- Create a tented feeling by hanging fabric from the ceiling.
- Paint the ceiling a darker color than the walls.

Too-Low Ceilings

- Paint the ceiling a lighter color than the walls.
- Take down anything hanging from the ceiling, including chandeliers.
- Make sure the scale of the furniture is right — high pieces do not belong in a low room.

No View or an Unattractive View

- Dress up bare walls.
- Add bright, vibrant landscapes: art can give you an urban view if you live in the country, and a vast and open view if you live in a bustling metropolis.
- Add beautiful window coverings so that you look at them rather than the view.
- Use mirrors to add light and a sense of openness.
- Focus the room away from the view by shifting the seating away from the windows.

Noisy Neighbors

- Install a small fountain to replace the neighbor noise with the soothing sound of trickling water.
- Keep beautiful background music on low all the time — I do this every day.

Awkward Room-to-Room Flow

- If you own your home, see an architect about removing a wall to encourage a loft-style feeling.
- If you rent, consider adding customized furniture pieces that suit the shape of your home — such as a built-in

bookcase or a bench sized for a nonstandard area —
instead of standard-sized pieces that may jut into hallways or block doorways.

Considering Color

When considering color choices, in addition to looking at palettes
and thinking about personal preference, I want you to think about
the ways that color can affect mood. Understanding the connection between color and emotion can help you make color choices
that can rev up a tired hallway or make a bedroom feel more like a
calm oasis. Keep in mind the following guidelines as you consider
which colors to incorporate in your SoulSpace.

ENERGETIC RED

Poppies, roses, poinsettia. Red stands for passion and heat,
strength and love. In China, it means celebration and luck, and
in India it means purity. If you want to add intensity — add red.

WARM ORANGE

Autumn leaves, ripe citrus, a sunset. Orange adds energy. A stim-
ulating color that brings warmth without the fiery overtones of
red, it can make a flamboyant statement. Not a color for the faint
of heart!

SUNNY YELLOW

Lemons, daisies, daffodils; happiness, hope, sunshine. Yellow
adds light to a space, adds brightness, adds charm. Great for
kitchens and children's bedrooms, yellow helps us learn and bol-
sters our confidence and creativity.

NATURAL GREEN

Grass, emeralds, a lush forest. Green stands for nature, for renewal, for youth and for spring, and it can make your home feel like a jewel box or a grassy meadow.

TRANQUIL BLUE

Ocean, sky, forget-me-nots. In Iran, blue is the color of heaven and spirituality, and in China, immortality. When you want to encourage a feeling of harmony and peace, of calm inspiration, look to blue.

POWERFUL PURPLE

Aubergines, banana flowers, orchids. Purple is royal and rich, noble and mysterious. For an air of sophistication and lush mystery, incorporate purple into your space.

PURE WHITE

Cumulus clouds, plumeria blossoms, lilies. White means purity and simplicity, but it also conjures feelings of summer, of winter, of innocence, of peace. And it serves as a great base for brighter colors.

DRAMATIC BLACK

The darkest skies, the deepest nights. Black is urbane and formal, elegant and always appropriate. Use this color in your home with discretion; overuse will be draining instead of dramatic.

GRACEFUL GRAY

Doves, platinum, the sky before it rains. Gray often stands for neutrality, but it is also timeless and dignified, a wonderful base color to incorporate into your home.

Cool Ivory

A white sand beach, a string of pearls. Quiet, pleasant, easy to get along with, cream may not be exciting on its own, but it offers a calm front that is easy to accessorize.

Rich Brown

A plowed field, chocolate truffles, a perfect espresso. Brown is earthy and outdoorsy, the rich feel of chocolate and coffee and the rich dirt from which all our food grows. Brown can be as lush and inviting indoors as out.

Revisiting Your Room-by-Room Assessment

In the first chapter, ASSESS, you spent a lot of time thinking about your home. In the chapters that followed, you created space and learned how to connect your dreams to your life. Now we use all that practical thinking and inspired dreaming to physically put the pieces together and make our SoulSpaces real. Now we take our "wants" and make them "haves."

Living Room

You now understand who uses your living room and what the purpose of the room is. If you learned that there is not adequate seating, you will use CREATE to achieve your goal of having a space where people can gather comfortably and spend time together. If you learned that your children use the living room more than you do and you want to take back your space, you will either turn an unused office into a playroom, or you will organize the living room so that everyone who wants to use it can do so happily.

Dining Room

By now, you've spent time sitting at the dining room table, paying attention at family gatherings, and doing whatever you need to, to understand the character of the room and how it might better serve you. Do you need to get a bigger table? Add a mirror to make the space feel larger? Get more comfortable chairs to encourage lingering at mealtimes? What can you add, subtract, or change to help the dining room live up to your dreams?

Kitchen

All the thinking you've done about your kitchen comes into play now. Cookbooks should be organized and within reach. Any missing cooking tools should be purchased and put away. If you determined that you needed a kitchen island, you've already gone shopping and found one that you love. Now bring it home and start enjoying it. If you've determined that new cabinets would make your kitchen shine, you've already called a contractor or placed an order.

Bathroom(s)

Was a Jacuzzi what you wanted? By now, you should have visited the showroom and be well on your way to installing it. Did you determine that adding an additional sink would make you and your partner less cranky in the mornings? What lighting changes did you decide your bathroom needed? Make them now.

Bedrooms

You've slept in your bedroom every night since you first assessed it. Now transform it. Lights, bedding, a new mattress: what did your assessment tell you that you needed? What did your dreams tell you that you needed? Bring in those elements, right now, today.

HOME OFFICE

We've already established how integral a proper home office is for getting your work done and feeling successful and professional. What did your assessment suggest your workspace needed? Has it all been ordered and/or installed? Pull the pieces out of the boxes and create your revitalized working space!

THE VIEW

What we see in our homes affects us; we have spent a lot of time considering the implications of this lesson. We have also considered the way that what we see outside our homes can impact the way we feel inside. Garden landscaping, window boxes, a tree placed strategically on a little city terrace — what we see outside always makes its way inside. How can you adjust your view so that it refreshes instead of distracting?

You've given a lot of thought to the passions that make you feel refreshed, inspired, and alive. Now make sure your home is infused with them. From a library covering your favorite subject matter to actual space to build, to paint, to dance, it's time to take your passions and really invite them in.

PART III

Living the Present

*"You must live in the present,
launch yourself on every wave,
find your eternity in each moment."*

— HENRY DAVID THOREAU

STAGE 7: ELEVATE
STAGE 8: CELEBRATE

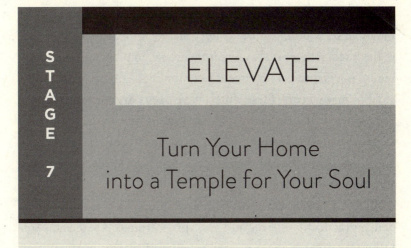

ELEVATE

Turn Your Home into a Temple for Your Soul

"When you have only two pennies left in the world,
buy a loaf of bread with one, and a lily with the other."

— CHINESE PROVERB

Every time I enter my home, I feel as if I am walking into a sacred temple, a place where my body, mind, and soul can rest from the busy day. I have consciously organized my SoulSpace so that it makes me feel cared for and supported. It allows me to let go of my day and slip easily into the comforts of the evening, whether I plan to be spending time alone or entertaining company.

When I walk through the door, soft instrumental music is playing, and I have the lights set on timers to go on when the natural light dims. Fresh flowers are placed around the house, and before I leave in the morning, I lay out my robe and slippers so they will be waiting for me when I arrive home. I make sure that in the kitchen there is always a little morsel to nibble on. After all, whose job is it to care for me if not mine?

For many years, these rituals have been part of my SoulSpace in Los Angeles. At Sowden House, I spent years creating a space to nourish and support my soul. I took time to collect items I love and cherish, and pulled them together into an ideal environment to soothe my soul and nourish my creativity.

Then I began work on the renovation project in Maui. Suddenly, practically overnight, I was thrust from this safe and carefully edited SoulSpace, a space in which I was in control of all the elements, into a very different lifestyle, with very different surroundings. Instead of opulence, Jason and I had bugs that took every open door as an invitation. Instead of a courtyard blooming with bougainvillea cultivated over years, we had a muddy expanse of soil. Instead of hand-picked fabrics, chosen for luxury and comfort, we were living in a beat-up bungalow in the middle of a construction site, struggling to create a semblance of home in this raw, unfinished space.

After months of work, we knew, this land would take its own gorgeous shape. But for a while we were basically camping out with hot running water. Armed with a list of numbers we pulled from Craigslist, with a big truck to put all our finds in, we set out to turn this temporary home into a place where we could flourish and evolve along with the property. A week, two weeks, a month in a space — any traveler or business nomad knows how quickly people root in a space and want to make it theirs, want to feel as if it is theirs. Just because it wouldn't be our home forever did not mean it was not our home right now.

Using Grace Notes to Elevate

Jason is magic when it comes to ELEVATE. He got out his broom and showed those bugs who was boss. He hung curtains so that we could have privacy. He covered the harsh lamps with fabric to soften the glow. He bought candles. He got inexpensive rugs for the doorways. He bought orchids and put them on the coffee tables. He bought incense and candles to light each night. And he always seemed to pick just the right music to play that fit with the environment we were living in. When he was done, it was as if someone had flipped a switch. Walking into this little bungalow, we didn't feel like homesteaders on the slope of a volcano; we felt as if we were home.

ELEVATE is a unique stage. Going through ASSESS or DREAM can take weeks or months. But ELEVATE is ongoing and can take only a moment — to hit "play" on your iTunes, to make the bed, to fluff the pillows. ELEVATE is packable, transportable, an ideal way to bring your SoulSpace with you on your next vacation or business trip as well as to turn your home into your temple, your sanctuary, your place of rest and renewal.

ELEVATE asks you to soften the edges with lights that dim. It encourages you to pack your suitcase with a loved photo, a scented candle, a familiar throw. It begs you to include little luxuries in your everyday life, from drinking glasses that feel great in your hand to a down pillow on the sofa that you can rest your head on in the evening. It teaches you to breathe life into your space by adding grace notes, the delicate touches that speak volumes.

Grace notes might include fresh flowers, from an individual, gorgeous bloom floating in a shallow bowl to an armful of wild-flowers found at the side of the road (or in your florist's shop); soft, pink lightbulbs that make everybody look younger and prettier, instantly; sheer curtains that add a layer of delicate privacy but still let the day glow through; a bowl full of nuts or chocolates; the sound of your favorite instrumental music playing low in the background. The details of luxury and comfort that might cost only a dollar yet make us feel as if we have been transported to a beautiful boutique hotel, grace notes can be music, candlelight, fabrics that make us feel cozy and snug, or scents that uplift and calm us.

Kari's Road Home

I met Kari at a fund-raising event for an organization that was helping her put her life back together again. Her story was a heart-wrenching one. She grew up in an abusive home, never feeling safe and protected by the adults who were supposed to take care of her. In order to escape this situation, she struck out on her own at fifteen, and her memoir, which she is working on, includes drugs, prostitution, homelessness, and jail.

After three years in prison, Kari was still a young woman in her midtwenties, and she knew it was time to make her life better. She looked for help, embraced sobriety, and enrolled in a course to hone her skills so that she could get a stable job. When I met Kari, she was not drinking or doing drugs, she had been working for a few months, and she had just been placed in an apartment.

When I visited Kari's apartment, she told me I was her first visitor. The ground-floor unit was sparsely furnished with very few personal items. The small yard was a square of dirt. It was clear that for all her progress, Kari was still struggling with the idea of having a home, not just a shelter. This was not surprising, especially considering how long it had been since Kari had really had a home. The house she grew up in had not felt like hers — so much so that she had run away. She had been in prison, which was not her home, although she was stuck there for three years. And a stint of homelessness, with no stable, steady place to lay her head each night, added to the confusion she must have been feeling now. Of course she did not know how to turn this bare apartment into a warm, safe den for herself — she had never experienced that! It was clear to me that my goal, and my challenge, was to introduce Kari to the idea of having a home — what it is, what it means, and what it could do for her.

As Kari and I spoke, I understood that she still didn't feel worthy of material possessions and was afraid that anything that belonged to her would be taken away. It was precisely this faith that I wanted her to have — the belief that she deserved things, and that in her new life she could have things that were really hers.

Before Kari and I could get to ELEVATE, we had a long road ahead of us. We spent a long time on ASSESS and RELEASE, dealing with where she was now and where she had been. While she didn't have many possessions to sift through, she had many strong memories and a lot of negative energy that had been poured into her by her family and her situation, and so in our CLEANSE stage, we had a smudging ceremony even though she thought it was silly. (She said this multiple times, using very colorful language, but she still participated. I left some of my sage sticks at her place, and the next time I came to her apartment, I could swear I smelled a hint of burned sage in the air...)

DREAM was a very important stage for Kari. Even though she had practice with this stage — if she hadn't dreamed of a better life for herself, she never would have had the fortitude to create it by seeking help, seeking knowledge, and seeking employment — she was not yet comfortable with the idea that if she wanted things in her life, she could dream them possible. DISCOVER was also a big one, since she had almost nothing. Her budget was tight even by thrift-store standards, so she drove around the neighborhood on days when people were throwing things out and managed to find some very cool old pieces that still had some life in them — for free! During CREATE, we discovered that she had a design ability that we were able to bring out by having her repair and refinish the furniture she'd found on her DISCOVER adventures.

HOME SWEET HOME

Then it was time for ELEVATE. Kari had been so good about all the stages, despite the great difficulty they posed for her — even the smudging ceremony! — that I was surprised by how reluctant she was to embrace ELEVATE. "What do I need a candle for?" she said. "I love my new home. I love what we've done. It's a sweet place now!"

She was right — it was a sweet place. The previously bare space now held shined and polished wooden furniture and a comfortable couch where she could relax at the end of the day. A painting she had found on one of her neighborhood explorations hung over the kitchen table. But to my eyes there was still something missing. All the furniture was there, and the dishes, and some artwork — but there was no extra life. No plants. No throws. No music. I could sit down, and I could eat a meal, but none of my senses were invigorated. There was nothing soft to touch. No delicate scent in the air. Nothing to listen to but the cars honking outside.

Details matter, I told her. A match struck to light a candle. A rug placed at an entryway. Delicious towels in the bathroom.

"That's silly," she responded. It was the sage all over again! Finally I realized that this was her SoulSpace, not mine, and decided to let it go. Still, being me, I couldn't completely let it go, not when it came to helping someone see how simple grace notes can turn a spare apartment into a sanctuary — so I sent her a beautiful scented candle as a housewarming gift.

Two weeks later, I got a sweet thank-you note, and an invitation. She wanted to talk to me about CELEBRATE, the final Soul-Space stage. She had met some new people at work, she said, and she wanted to have them over.

Home Sweeter Home

When I got to Kari's house, I was in for a shock. It was completely transformed. There was a sunflower in a large glass vase in the corner of the entryway. The back of her couch had a soft cotton throw on it. Joan Baez's voice lilted in the air. In the yard, a row of tulips stood brightly against the raw wood fencing, and she'd also planted a small patch of greens and herbs. And on the coffee table that she had found and polished, the candle I sent her was lit, releasing a soft lavender scent into the air.

"Wow," I said. "Wow." I must have said that about ten times.

Kari laughed, delighted with the effect her efforts toward ELEVATE had inspired. And I was delighted to hear what had finally inspired her efforts: it was the candle I sent her.

"There was some electrical problem in the building the day the candle arrived," she said. "Right before I was about to take a shower, the lights went out. But I had to go to a meeting; I couldn't wait. So I used the candle. It changed everything. Suddenly, I wasn't in a tiny bathroom, annoyed because of the lights. I was somewhere else. Somewhere special. Somewhere I really wanted to be. When the lights came back on I was actually *upset*."

Those moments, bathing in the warm water in the soft glow of a candle, with the scent of lavender in the air, were a catalyst for Kari. They showed her that luxury isn't always about big-ticket items, that it can be about affordable treats that turn everyday activities into special pleasures. This experience inspired her to elevate other areas of her apartment by incorporating flowers, music, and textures that made her feel wonderful, and truly at home.

Nourishing All Your Senses

Many of the SoulSpace stages involve big thinking and big changes. Letting go is hard; so is dreaming big. ELEVATE, on the other hand, focuses on the *small* shifts that transform a house into a home by nourishing all your senses, conscious design that inspires unconscious relaxation. A vase full of lilies on the table. Fresh fruit in the kitchen. A clean towel set out for guests, and a pitcher of cool water at a bedside. Curtains draped over windows. A cashmere wrap on the back of a sofa, waiting to make you feel instantly cozy and warm. We're trying not to overwhelm the senses but to relieve them, to provide a safe space against the backdrop of the busy, hectic world.

All our senses need to be engaged and vibrant in order for us to achieve all that we desire on a soul level. Each of our senses can feed us on a profound level: we can eat color, taste sight, remember past experiences through scent, be deeply moved emotionally through sound, and have the most profound *ahhh* feeling through touch. It's time to wake up our senses, which can support us in creating everything our hearts desire. We have all been dulled down by our patterns and routines. With ELEVATE, we engage the passion that lives inside us by adding external prompts that will help us manifest all our dreams.

ELEVATE doesn't take a lot of effort, but it imbues a great deal of meaning — for you and for your family and friends. ELEVATE

makes us feel welcomed, cared for, and loved. In this transforma-
tive stage, you take the space you have created and honor it. By
doing so, you also honor yourself and the people with whom you
share your home.

SIGHT

What we see can inspire us like nothing else. Imagine driving
and coming to a vista where it seems as if you can see forever,
or looking at a piece of art that thrills your soul. You can help
expand your sense of belonging and connection by understanding the ways that what you see moves you — and by making sure
that you are moved deeply by the way you have organized and
presented the visual aspects of your home.

What we see imprints itself in our minds, sending us subtle
suggestions about mood and setting. You've spent all this time to
create your ideal environment — now you must double-check for
visual inconsistencies that might be jarring. Here are some tips
for making your SoulSpace a feast for the eyes.

- Make sure art is hung at eye level. Many people hang their
  art too high or too low, which makes it feel as if it is floating or sinking. Some people recommend 57 inches from
  the ground, which is "gallery height," but if the members
  of your household are very tall or petite, you'll want to
  adjust accordingly so that you and those you live with can
  enjoy your art.
- There is lighting for tasks — bright! — and lighting for
  romance — dim! There is lighting to illuminate and lighting to allure, lighting so that you can read your book and
  lighting so that you can see your plate. Most people have
  one kind of lighting in their homes. We all have many

different moods and ways of being in our homes, and lighting is an important way to transition between different moods. Instead of lights on or lights off, try layering with overheads, lamps, and candles so that you can increase or decrease brightness as needed. Using dimmers wherever possible is a fine way to control the light for the situations in which you will use them.

- Window coverings are another wonderful way to adjust the mood in your home. Sheers and drapes, pleated shades and shutters — I look for coverings that allow for privacy but still allow the light to flow into and light up the room.

SOUND

If you live near the ocean, a waterfall, or a bird sanctuary, you are lucky because your ears are constantly being fed lovely and relaxing tones. If you go to sleep listening to crickets, you already have a bit of ELEVATE in your home. If you wake up listening to roosters, you already know that not all winged creatures sing a soothing song...

You can incorporate many sounds into your environment that are more pleasing than the thud of a neighbor's hammer, the barking of a far-off (but not far-enough-off) dog, or the stop-start of traffic. In Maui, we are awakened by the call of the roosters and occasionally the scream of a visiting mynah bird. During our construction phase, Jason and I were staying in a unit right by the road, where we heard cars passing all day. In order to separate our tidy little home from the activity around us, we planted a row of tall ginger flowers and bought a little fountain for fifty dollars on Craigslist that would stream constantly, creating a water sound that was much more relaxing and pleasant than the whoosh of trucks riding up the slope of the volcano. How can you fill your home with sweet sounds?

- When adding sound to your home, try to replace jarring sounds — like street traffic or the neighbor's television set — with more ambient tones, like soft music.
- Those who do live near the ocean may have noticed that when we get used to a certain sound we stop hearing it actively — it becomes white noise. If you've stopped noticing the sounds inherent in your home, change it up! Experiment with sounds to see how they make you feel: rock music and wind chimes have very different effects on the soul.
- A water element, such as a fountain in a backyard, can create a pleasing sound that may not drown out other noise but will give you something else to listen to! You can also purchase recordings of the sounds of nature — from birds calling to a river rushing — from many stores and other venues.
- Your favorite CD is always a good choice. Jason makes sure we have soft, ambient music playing in our home because he says I need to relax more, and relaxing tones help me slip off some of the pressures of the day as soon as I step in the door.
- Some people enjoy the sound of chimes hung on a porch or by a window; others would rather do without. Whatever you like is what you should incorporate!

TOUCH

Touch is about physical comfort. This is the sense that involves your whole body, from the way a texture feels on your skin to the way your entire self settles into the couch or stretches across your mattress. Touch is one of the most important senses we have, which is why luxury fabrics — such as cashmere, fur, velvet, and deep plush carpeting and rugs — do something profound to us and make us feel taken care of, abundant, deep, comforted.

Do you wear slippers in your home or do you walk around barefoot? If you wear slippers, are they soft and comfortable, a haven for your toes? If you walk around barefoot, what are the floors in your home like? Are they a pleasure to walk on? Are they smooth and cool? Are they slippery? Are they swept daily, or vacuumed as often as necessary?

What about your sheets, your towels, and the robe you put on after your shower? We touch the things in our homes, all the time, and they touch us back. Don't you want them to be soft, clean, and of the finest quality you can afford?

• Incorporate comfortable textures into your flooring wherever possible. Rugs and carpets are a wonderful way to let your feet know you have entered a different part of your house. A shag carpet can be especially fun to walk around on. At Sowden House, the guest bathroom floor is made of smooth stones that rise up from their mooring. A visiting friend told me that bathroom was her favorite room in the house, just because of how happy her feet were to walk around on that floor.

• Linens are an important vehicle for touch. A higher thread count means softer sheets, so pay attention! You want 300 or more, ideally. Blankets are also key, especially if you live in colder climates, not only in the bedroom but also in the living room and the den. A few throws of cashmere, wool, silk, or cotton tucked into a convenient spot will make chilly people very happy very soon.

- Pillows and cushions also encourage touch. When you rest your head or your back against a pillow, it is literally supporting you, holding you up so that your muscles can let go and relax. Make sure you have ample cushions that don't just look good but also feel good!

Scent

From lovely perfumes spritzed on before we leave the house in the morning to the freshly baked donuts at the bakery around the corner from the office to the spicy curry at the dinner table — morning, noon, and evening, our noses are subjected to an onslaught of delicate fragrances and pungent odors.

Using scent to support us can be a powerful way to elevate. Give all your sensibilities a treat when you step through the door, making sure your environment is fresh and tidy and full of delicious aromas so you can really stop and smell the jasmine. Here are some of my favorite ways to incorporate scent.

- Flowers are a treat for the eyes and for the nose. Especially fragrant blooms include tuberoses, lilies, roses, and jasmine. Have you ever noticed how a subtle scent can bring back memories in an explosive way? Every year on my mother's birthday, I buy gardenias. She loved gardenias, and her perfume was scented with their fragrance. When I surround myself with gardenias, I feel my mother all around me.
- I love candles scented with natural oils, not only for the delicate glow they cast in a room — instant elevation! — but for the delicate aromas that linger in rooms where they are used regularly. The scent of the ocean calms me deeply, so when I want to feel relaxed, I burn a candle scented like the sea.

- Aromatherapy diffusers are another lovely way to incorporate scent into your home design. Fill the reservoir with some water and a few drops of your favorite essential oil, light the candle underneath, and voilà!

SCENT BY ROOM

- In the dining room, make sure that scents complement food and will not overwhelm what you are serving: a light lemon or rosemary scent is more appropriate than something heavy or floral.
- In the kitchen, scent can anchor us: baking bread or cake is a wonderful way to feel more at home, not only for the delicious treat but also for the scent of baked goods rising through your home. I have memories of my mother roasting brisket in the oven for hours. To me brisket is the ultimate comfort food because even the scent makes me feel comforted. So every once in a while I put a brisket in the oven, especially when I need to feel truly at home.

  Keep kitchens smelling fresh all the time by making sure to keep garbage out of sight and out of mind. Take the trash out frequently and store garbage bins far from common and eating areas.
- The bathroom is a wonderful place to include scent. When you're washing up, you want to feel fresh and clean, so a fresh, clean scent is a natural choice for the bathroom.
- In the bedroom, where you may want to encourage feelings of romance, look for floral scents such as rose or jasmine.
- The office is a place where we want to feel invigorated and focused: try cinnamon, which will wake up your senses.

TASTE

Taste links us to the world. Have you seen little children who try to put everything in their mouths? It's because taste is one of our instinctual methods for exploring our universe.

Consider the difference between a fast-food burger and a dinner cooked by someone who appreciates the subtle wonder of flavor. How do you feel while eating the fast food? Do you linger over your white flour bun and exclaim about the delicious sesame seeds? Or do you cram it into your face and then move on to the next thing? How about the sumptuously cooked dinner? You might enjoy it course by course, paired with wine, noticing how the fresh thyme makes the sauce sing, how the crème brûlée has the delicate flavor of lavender.

Use the powers of taste to elevate your home environment, your life, and yourself. You don't have to hire a Michelin-starred chef to cook your dinner every night; you just need a bowl of fresh fruit on the kitchen table and a sense of wonder and curiosity.

- If you see a strange fruit at the market, bring it home. Trying a new food keeps our taste buds and our attention sharp, subtly tugging us out of ingrained patterns. Unusual fruits and vegetables remind us that we have not tried everything in the world yet and that we need to stay open to new experiences and possibilities — to taste more from the tree of life.
- Stop saving for a special occasion. If you're a romantic and you love chocolate-covered strawberries, why wait for a lover to deliver them? Indulge your sense of taste on a regular basis and elevate your experience of taste within your home.

- Slip slices of cucumber or citrus, plus herbs, into your filtered water pitcher for refreshing changes of taste. Try cucumber and mint, or orange and rosemary, or lemon, lime, and basil.
- Add fresh herbs to your cooking routine — try growing pots of basil, mint, parsley, chives, or rosemary on a windowsill for an always-fresh feast for the eyes as well as the taste buds.

EXERCISE: ADD GRACE

The ELEVATE stage is about feeling as though you live in a really plush place no matter how big or small your home is. Embrace the rich comfort and abundance that is available to you all the time, whether through taste, smell, sight, feel, or sound. All your senses should be engaged when you get home.

For this exercise, make it your mission to incorporate at least one grace note for each of your senses in each room. Remember, we aren't trying to make your home feel and smell like an Indian bazaar, with a different scent or sound or texture in every corner; rather, we want all your senses to be gently cared for, so your soul can settle.

The Four Elements

Fire, earth, water, air: a true SoulSpace needs to have all the elements of nature in balance. Modern life often removes us from these elements, and by bringing them into our homes, we deepen our connection to the natural world, and our knowledge that we are of nature and of the elements.

Fire

Fire ignites the passion that lives inside us. It nourishes the spirit, feeds the soul, and reconnects us to our most potent energies. Cuddling with a loved one near a fire is not only romantic but rejuvenating. Gathering family and friends at an outdoor campfire awakens something primal within us. Eating by candlelight reminds us to pause, consider, and appreciate. Passion is often described as a "fire in the belly." The passion that comes from fire is missing or quieted down in most of us. We all need to find the fire, which can give us the energy we need to make the changes we want to make.

- Incorporating the fire element in your bedroom can help you connect to your most fiery passions and their expression. A row of flickering candles ignites passion as well as shifting the familiar into something that moves, that changes, that excites.
- Painting the walls in semigloss colors of orange, red, and yellow reflects light and energy.
- A vase of fresh flowers with all the colors of flames — reds, oranges, yellows — can also suggest the element of fire.
- Add fire spirit without lighting a match: use up-lights in the corners of rooms to capture and focus light energy.

Earth

The earth has so much to say to us; often we are not listening, and yet she is always speaking. Everything — every rock, every leaf, even the wind — can carry a message. Generations ago we lived much closer to the earth. We listened and watched as the seasons changed. We were connected to the times of harvesting and planting.

Everything has a season. Too often we try to rush the births of things, even our dreams. Surrounding yourself with elements of the earth in your home — from imagery of mountainscapes and fields to plants, rocks, and crystals — will connect you to your true nature and make your home feel more alive.

If you have ever stood in the middle of a redwood grove or another deep forest, you understand the power of Mother Nature. She is here to support us; we just need to bring her home.

- Make sure that you have living plants growing in your space. Whether or not you have a green thumb, there is a plant out there that is just for you! Visit your local nursery, and they will be able to direct you to the perfect plant for your home and needs.
- You can also decorate your home with beautiful rocks or crystals, such as pieces of amethyst or quartz, which bring in the earth element and make exquisite accessories. I have crystals all over my house because they are beautiful and because on an unconscious level I know that they come from deep within the earth, and they remind me to stay grounded and connected while my imagination is free to take flight.

Water

The water element teaches us about flow and balance. Rain falls, becomes rivers, and evaporates to form clouds, which become rain. Rivers lead us to open waters. Water moves, it travels, it can be contained in a vessel, but only for so long.

When you tip a bowl with water in it, the water pours out of the bowl. Water shows how important balance is if we want to retain what we have, if we don't want our essence to rush out along the floorboards...

There are no hard edges in water, reminding us that there should be no hard edges within us.

- Spending time in or near water is crucial to our inner balance, as is drinking plenty of fresh water every day. Keep a glass pitcher of water on your nightstand, along with a glass.
- Incorporate water into your home via a swimming pool, a Jacuzzi, steam, a fountain, an aquarium, or even a bowl full of stones and water.
- Our bodies crave immersion. Your daily shower or bath can reconnect you to your watery origins if you take the time to breathe and meditate between soaping and rinsing. A bath by candlelight adds both fire and water elements to your SoulSpace experience.

Air

The air surrounds us, all the time, touching our skin and our faces, filling our lungs, keeping us alive. The wind blows by our faces, carrying with it pollen from a neighbor's tree, oxygen from the nearby plants, moisture from this morning's rain.

On your way to fulfilling your dreams and elevating your SoulSpace, you need to be able to breathe deeply, to truly take in the breath of life, filling your body, your entire body, with the sweetness of clean air. Breathing deeply to take in the air helps us have a deeper and a more supported experience in this life.

Keeping the air in your home fresh and clean is integral.

- Open windows to let the air in.
- Use fans to encourage circulation.
- Use all-natural cleaning products to keep things fresh (see pages 88–90).
- Scented candles and fresh flowers make air sweet to smell.
- Lots of green plants will help purify the air in your home.

EXERCISE: ADD THE ELEMENTS

Make sure to incorporate at least one significant example of each element in your home to keep your home in balance with nature. Too much or not enough of an element can make an environment feel "off." When your elements are properly represented, you can be inside and still be connected to the primal parts of your being.

This exercise could be as extensive as remodeling your courtyard (air) to include a Jacuzzi (water), a fire pit (fire), and an edible garden (earth). Or it could be as simple as adding a scented candle (fire and air) and a bamboo plant in a clear vase full of water with stones at the bottom (earth and water).

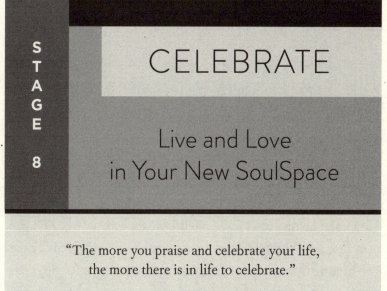

CELEBRATE

Live and Love
in Your New SoulSpace

"The more you praise and celebrate your life,
the more there is in life to celebrate."

— OPRAH WINFREY

The conversation I had with Kari after she had showed me her apartment, elevated and softened by the grace notes she had added, revolved around her new interest in sharing (and showing off) her space to her new and growing community. By making shifts that encouraged her renewal, from quitting drugs and expanding her education; by asking for help and changing her circumstances; by taking a real interest in her surroundings, her dreams, and her hopes for herself — she was able to experience real hopefulness and satisfaction. Now she was ready for others to recognize and appreciate how far she had come, how much she had to offer herself and the world. It was time to expand and ask her friends for support in her newfound life.

Celebrate Yourself

There are so many ways to celebrate, and it is one thing in life that we don't do enough of. I believe that we are here to be in joy and to enjoy. We remember to complain, and we remember to pick up the dry cleaning, but we forget to celebrate life, our work, our family, our friends, ourselves. Celebrating is a way of giving thanks and being grateful for the life we have. Use everything as an excuse to celebrate! We are here for such a short period of time. Celebrating is so simple, and yet we so often forget. It brings us a lot of joy, and joy gives us a lot more passion, and passion is what fulfills our dreams.

Before you invite others in for a large (or intimate) gathering, I recommend taking some time to fully appreciate your renewed space by yourself or with those you live with. In Kari's case, the small garden she had planted in her yard was in bloom, giving her access to fresh lettuces and some herbs. She had always wanted to learn to cook, so she bought a cookbook that a friend had recommended highly, and set out to prepare a delicious, healthful dinner for herself. That evening at home, eating a meal she had cooked, prefaced by a salad of greens that she had grown herself, nourished her more than a meal cooked by the finest chef in the finest restaurant with the rarest truffles on the planet ever could have.

It was so important for her to connect to her space and feel the way it was enriching her life. Home is the one place in the world where we have the control to create an environment that makes us feel safe and nurtured. It is the foundation for your life — a place that is always waiting for you with an open door.

Once you have completed the first seven stages, it's important to celebrate all you have accomplished. Sit back or walk around with a glass of wine or a cup of tea, and truly take in all the beauty you have created.

Celebrate Your Community

Once Kari had celebrated her new SoulSpace on her own, making herself feel truly at home in the process, she was ready to invite others in to share her new good fortune. Her twenty-eighth birthday was approaching, so she decided to host a celebration at which she could honor the person she had become, thanks to the support of the people she had decided to make her family.

Kari turned out to be a natural hostess, as gracious and elegant as if she had been instructed by teachers at the most exclusive finishing schools. She served us simple appetizers and toasted pitas, hummus, and crudités alongside large platters of cheese and olives. If anyone was a stranger to the rest of her guests, she offered a small introduction to make sure they felt at home in her home.

Kari really impressed me. I was taken with her spirit, with her courage, and with the natural ease she had discovered when she was finally at home — really, truly at home. If Kari can do it, any of us can do it. She took a difficult string of circumstances and turned her life around. She went from having no home of her own to having a cozy, well-decorated abode that made her feel safe enough to open her door — and her heart — to the possibility that people were good, were kind, and were loving. By inviting them to celebrate with her, in her home, she showed them that she trusted them enough to let them in — literally. And the community she found showed her that her trust was, finally, well placed.

When you bring friends and family in to celebrate the new-found you and your new SoulSpace, you are creating a larger net-work of support on the road to manifesting your dreams, hopes, and wishes for your life. When you have yourself, your space, and your intimate community supporting you, you start feeling as if you can accomplish anything.

It can be scary to expose yourself and your renewed home to your friends and your community, but believe me, it's well worth it. We need all the support we can get as we work to fulfill our dreams.

The more you connect to your home — to the true creative expression of you — the safer it will become to share yourself with others in your home. The more peace we find at home, the more peace we can offer to the world.

Write Your Own Happy Ending

Brian came to LA with dreams of making it big as a screenwriter, but a few years into his time on the West Coast, instead of driving around in a Bentley and thanking all the little people at awards shows, he was working at a copy shop and any other jobs that came his way. His greatest writing success to date was a screen-writing award he had won after college. Now his dreams were rapidly deflating because he was finding it nearly impossible to break through.

I took Brian on as a client because I was taken by his optimis-tic attitude. While others might have given up, Brian was stead-fast. "I don't care how many pages I have to collate," he told me, breathless because he had dashed outside to chat while he was on a ten-minute break at work. "I don't care how many pages I have to staple together. I know that I have a talent. I know that if I can get the right eyes on my work, if I can keep writing, I'm going to break through."

I thought that Brian's attitude demonstrated a mature understanding of his talent. So many of us live in a world of apologies, where we package our creative endeavors in a litany of "it's probably terrible" and "just tell me if you hate it" instead of telling the world, "I wrote this, and I think it is great." Why should the world accept you if you don't accept yourself? With this thinking, I assured Brian, he was exactly the kind of person I wanted to work with.

When I got to his one-bedroom apartment, I was no longer sure. He slept on a futon, there was a layer of dust on everything, comics were strewn about, and all he had in the fridge was takeout. He also didn't have a dedicated place to write and ended up occasionally pecking away on his laptop in bed or in front of the TV. It looked as if he was suffering from a certain amount of arrested development, and the immaturity I saw reflected in his space made me wonder if his perception of his abilities was more about not facing the truth than about being committed to his ideals.

Some of the tasks at hand were clear and came through almost immediately in the initial stages of our SoulSpace process. We agreed that he needed to keep a weekly checklist of household chores to accomplish, at least until he could afford a housekeeper to come in once a week and scare away the dust mice. By becoming accountable for his space, he would be able to feel better about having people over, which was one of the goals he had expressed at our first meeting.

"I don't really have any friends," he confessed once we were seated on his futon. "I used to have loads of buddies, but we hung out in bars and clubs. Now everyone is engaged or married. All they want to do is hang out at each other's houses and have dinner. They used to invite me. I stopped going: I never had a place to invite them back to."

Work was another area where Brian clearly needed to take control. We turned a huge walk-in closet into an office where he could work in a dedicated place. We placed his screenwriting award prominently on a shelf to remind him of his potential.

CELEBRATE was an integral part of Brian's SoulSpacing on a number of levels. When I told him that I thought he needed to have a personal celebration before he opened his new home to others, he got it right away. "There's a big game on Sunday!" he said. "I'll get a six pack and really kick back!"

This was exactly what I had *not* envisioned. I encouraged him to cook dinner for himself and eat at the new space-saver table we had installed (a plank of wood on a hinge so it could be lifted up to conserve space when necessary). We compromised — he agreed to get some delicious Thai takeout and eat it at his new table.

EXERCISE: CELEBRATE WITH YOURSELF AND WITH YOUR HOUSEHOLD

The first step to enjoying your new SoulSpace is to celebrate with yourself. Even if you live with others, if you have been the driving force behind the renewal of your home, you deserve a treat all to yourself!

It can be a carefully prepared dinner...or breakfast in bed and a morning sleeping in. It doesn't matter! Doing whatever makes you feel good is how you should celebrate in your new SoulSpace.

Once you feel fully connected to the space, plan an evening with the members of your household. Let everyone fully embrace and enjoy the home that you will be sharing.

Open Your Home to Fresh Opportunities

After Brian had broken in the new space by celebrating on his own, it was time to invite others to share it. First, he invited his old friends whom he had not seen in ages — to watch the game. This was the perfect occasion for the group, who enjoyed the wings and beers he provided. They were able to reconnect, he was able to have them at his home, and he neatly sidestepped the issue of a formal sit-down dinner. By avoiding a more formal arrangement, he had left room for one of them to bring a new friend to the party, a pretty young woman whom Brian felt an immediate spark with.

The next celebration Brian hosted was less of a party and more of a gathering that would inspire creativity and community. He had become acquainted with a few other screenwriters, so he invited them to start a writing group with him where they could all bounce ideas off one another. They met weekly at each other's homes, with the launch meeting hosted by Brian. Having his old friends over had given him a new confidence, and he was happy to report to me that this informal writer's group ultimately became a great support system. Eventually, they turned the coffee-and-donuts gatherings into potluck dinners, started inviting actors, and were able to do readings of their work, which gave them all a lot of pleasure.

When I heard all of this, I was so happy for Brian, who had used his refinished apartment to reconnect with his old frien and make some great new ones. But I worried about his career dreams. Many months later, he called to tell me that he had still not sold a screenplay and that he was going to give up on his dream of writing a movie, at least for a while.

"I'm so sorry," I said. This was honestly not the outcome I had expected. "What are you going to do instead?"

"I'm throwing a party!" he told me. "I got a job writing for television!"

Celebrate the Milestones

When we are children, our parents cheer for all our accomplishments. Color a picture? You're an artist. Tie your shoes? You're a genius. Have a birthday? You're the star.

As we get older, such praise is not always forthcoming. Even when we know we have achieved something incredible, whether it's passing a difficult exam, learning to ride a skateboard, or, yes, having a birthday, the world often doesn't take notice. Even our partners, friends, and children might not be waiting at the door, cake in hand, when we get a promotion, write a brilliant letter to the editor, or finish our first 10k run. Just as we arrange our homes to support our success and joy, we have to arrange our schedules to honor those same things when we hit the goals we set for ourselves — and we have to invite others to share in our good fortune, just as we enjoy helping them honor their own commitments and achievements.

When I turned fifty, I made up my mind that this year I would really celebrate. Fifty felt like a big deal to me, so I decided to honor it by throwing a big party. Also, this birthday happened to coincide with the finish of the big renovation I did at Sowden House, and the timing seemed perfect: I wanted to celebrate the person I had become and the people who supported me, and I could do so while sharing the redesign of my space, so that my friends and family could see and feel the outward manifestation of my personal transformation.

I had gone through all the SoulSpace stages while working on this redesign, and now it was time to relax and revel in all the hard work I had put into mining my psyche and creating this beautiful space, this renewed space that was the perfect complement to my older and hopefully wiser self. This type of celebration is integral because it is not just an honoring — it is an opportunity. This was my chance to enroll the loving support system I needed to continue to build the new me, to continue to make those shifts and adjustments that would keep me on course.

Instead of physical gifts, I invited my friends to bring an expression of their artistry or creativity. My friend Trey, an amazing dance choreographer, runs a company that specializes in stilt dancing. Trey arrived at the celebration dressed as the character Pan and did a beautiful dance routine, to my delight and the applause of all the guests. My dear friend Maggy, an opera singer, sang in Italian. Others recited poetry. This was the most amazing event I had ever participated in, as either a host or an invited guest, because it was cocreated with so much heart, love, and creativity.

For me, the most magical moment of the celebration was when Jason stood at the piano and sang for all of us. In my six years of living with and loving Jason, I had heard him sing only once before. His voice is magical and healing, a rare gift that he sometimes blesses others with.

As soon as Jason began, as the first bars of "Grateful" by John Bucchino floated over the room, the crowd, who had been up on their feet, out of their seats, laughing and calling to one another, fell completely silent. Every ounce of energy in that room was focused on Jason. I was in tears from the moment he started to sing.

What a beautiful celebration of life, and of home! I was home in a deeper way than I had ever been before.

Honor Community Efforts

The SoulSpace process starts with you and your home, then moves out into your support system of friends and family and then to the community at large. CELEBRATE is about giving and sharing, about creating a safe, stable, beautiful space for yourself to help give you the resilience of spirit to deal with all the challenges that exist in the world. I almost always have celebrations and events in my home rather than out at a restaurant or alternative space because I always want to infuse my events with love and a deep sense of intimacy.

I often host events and parties at my home in Los Angeles in cooperation with local and national nonprofits, lending my home to these causes so they can attract a larger crowd: everybody seems to want a glimpse of Lloyd Wright's architecture. This kind of celebration is ideal if you're not comfortable putting yourself in the spotlight. By focusing the attention on a cause that you would like to help further, you can share your home, do something good for your community, and have a great time.

EXERCISE: CELEBRATE WITH YOUR COMMUNITY

After you have connected with yourself and your space, it's time to invite others in. SoulSpace has helped me truly find my home, not only in the spaces I occupy, but within myself. Over the course of this journey, you have become more intimate with yourself and your space. Now is the time to become more intimate with the world that lives around you.

CONCLUSION

Welcome Home

Welcome home. It truly is a new day.

Now that you have completed this process, now that your mind is accustomed to seeing what is really there and to tapping into your creative energy, I hope you will carry the Soul-Space process into all the corners of your life.

As you grow and change, as your desires evolve, you will naturally examine and restore your surroundings, keeping your SoulSpace up-to-date with your soul. Take your time! One step at a time! This process will serve you for your entire life. It isn't about how long it takes you; all that matters is that you start.

You can live in the most beautiful way possible — and you deserve to. Your soul is waiting for you to connect with it and express yourself so that you can truly see and share who is living inside you. Be beautiful. Be you to the fullest — that is the greatest beauty.

Forget about other people's styles. What do you love about yourself? What do you want to learn about yourself? What parts of your soul need to be expressed and set free into the world?

Find what you love! Find your voice! Find yourself! Your SoulSpace is your safe haven, the place where you can experiment, explore, and express yourself. It is a laboratory of you! Move the couch a hundred times if you have to, until it feels just right. You will know it when it is — it will just be a resounding yes!

So, please, trust yourself. Try different things. When new journeys begin, such as a new relationship or a new job, you will find that things need to shift and change in your surroundings. Hermit crabs must change shells as they grow, or they will die; we humans also need our shells to change as we grow...

Let your space be a breathing, living entity that shifts and changes with you. In this way, it will stay fresh — and you will stay inspired. Let the interior design of your home be an extension of the interior design of you. When the outside of you and the inside of you are in harmony, you will find peace.

So be at home and reach out to all that you love — connected to your soul and the space in which you live. Creating space for your soul is the greatest gift you can give yourself.

Welcome to your new home and your new life,
Xorin

ACKNOWLEDGMENTS

My thanks go to my family, not only the family that I was born into but the family that I have chosen in my life: my mother, Selma, who has already passed; my father, Henry; my brothers, Craig and Barry; my life partner, Jason; and my brother from another mother, Norman, for always believing in me and reminding me of my potential in the moments of my forgetfulness. Without all of you, I would not be who I am and who you have come to know. Specifically, I would like to acknowledge Jason for being my grounding rod and putting up with all my insecurities while writing this book, until those insecurities became transformed into trust and a deep state of inner peace.

I thank Henry Bloomstein for working with me initially to organize all my thoughts and material in preparation for writing this book. My thanks go to Noam Dromi for not only believing in the Soulspace process but assisting me on so many levels to get this book published. I would also like to thank my agents at William Morris Endeavor, Ivo Fisher and Rebecca Oliver. Rebecca, thank you for believing in this book and finding its right publishing home.

Thank you to Georgia Hughes, my editor at New World Library, for trusting and loving this book from the very beginning, and my copyeditor, Kristen Cashman, for all your amazing feedback in the editing process — you brought a lot of clarity to the final structure.

Most of all, I would like to thank Sandra Bark, my cowriter and friend, for giving your time, your heart, and your soul to this book, for believing that I had something important to share, for believing that I had a book inside me that wanted to express itself, and for all the hard work you put into the creation of this book. Thank you for being the perfect person for me to work with to help me express the words and the inspiration that I so wanted to share with others.

Marianne Williamson, who wrote the most beautiful words in the foreword, I am so grateful for your friendship and your generosity in your words.

And thank you to God, the source of all life, for guiding me into my true life's work. Mahalo to all of you, from my SoulSpace in Maui.

INDEX

ABOUT THE AUTHOR

Xorin Balbes is an award-winning architectural conservator, designer, philanthropist, and co-owner of the interior and architectural design firm SoulSpace Home (formerly Temple-Home). The company is well known for its remarkable restorations of several architecturally significant properties in the Los Angeles area, including the Sowden House, a 1926 Lloyd Wright–designed home; Talmadge Villa, the Los Feliz replica of a seventeenth-century Italian villa and the former home of 1920s screen legend Norma Talmadge; and the 1929 art deco Security First National Bank. SoulSpace Home's most recent undertaking is the restoration of the Fred Baldwin Memorial Home, an adaptive reuse project that is opening as the newest destination on Maui's North Shore. This rejuvenation sanctuary, which will be called SoulSpace Sanctuary, is on six private acres and has twenty-eight bedrooms, all with ocean views, and a farm-to-table restaurant. The principles of the SoulSpace process have been incorporated throughout the restoration.

Xorin's thirty-nine impressive redesigns and renovations as a real estate developer and interior designer encouraged him to develop his own philosophy for home design, which he calls Soul-Space. His work and TempleHome have been featured extensively in publications including *Architectural Digest*, *Wallpaper* magazine, *Traditional Home*, *Metropolitan Home*, and *The Robb Report*, as well as in a variety of television profiles on Home and Garden Television, *Entertainment Tonight*, and many other programs and networks.

Xorin is also the cofounder of the nonprofit organization Global Vision for Peace, which launched at the 2002 Academy Awards, with many prominent celebrities and Oscar winners sending a message to the world that Americans were standing up for peace. The organization's focus and mission have recently evolved to promote awareness of and solutions to the burgeoning problem of homelessness, focusing on one person, one family at a time.

Xorin divides his time between his Los Angeles and Maui offices of SoulSpace Home. Additionally, he is overseeing the creation of SoulSpace Sanctuary on Maui. His website is www.SoulSpaceHome.com.

NEW WORLD LIBRARY is dedicated to publishing books and other media that inspire and challenge us to improve the quality of our lives and the world.

We are a socially and environmentally aware company, and we strive to embody the ideals presented in our publications. We recognize that we have an ethical responsibility to our customers, our staff members, and our planet.

We serve our customers by creating the finest publications possible on personal growth, creativity, spirituality, wellness, and other areas of emerging importance. We serve New World Library employees with generous benefits, significant profit sharing, and constant encouragement to pursue their most expansive dreams.

As a member of the Green Press Initiative, we print an increasing number of books with soy-based ink on 100 percent postconsumer-waste recycled paper. Also, we power our offices with solar energy and contribute to nonprofit organizations working to make the world a better place for us all.

Our products are available
in bookstores everywhere.
For our catalog, please contact:

New World Library
14 Pamaron Way
Novato, California 94949

Phone: 415-884-2100 or 800-972-6657
Catalog requests: Ext. 50
Orders: Ext. 52
Fax: 415-884-2199
Email: escort@newworldlibrary.com

To subscribe to our electronic newsletter, visit
www.newworldlibrary.com